WritingLands

WritingLands

Composing with Old and New Writing Tools

Jane Zeni
University of Missouri–St. Louis

National Council of Teachers of English
1111 Kenyon Road, Urbana, Illinois 61801

To the Members of the Gateway Writing Project

Staff Editor: Robert A. Heister

Cover Design: Doug Burnett

Interior Book Design: Tom Kovacs for TGK Design

NCTE Stock Number: 59036–3020

Library of Congress Cataloging in Publication Data

Zeni, Jane, 1945–
     WritingLands : composing with old and new writing tools / Jane
Zeni.
        p. cm.
     Includes bibliographical references (p.   ).
     ISBN 0–8141–5903–6
     1. English language—Composition and exercises—Study and teaching
(Secondary)   2. English language—Rhetoric—Study and teaching.
I. Title.
PE1404.45   1990
808'.042'0712—dc20   90–6557
                                                                              CIP

Contents

Acknowledgments

This book is the product of collaborative learning. All the teachers whose classrooms I describe have participated in St. Louis's Gateway Writing Project, and most have studied with me in the Graduate Invitational Institutes. They have published articles, written grant proposals, and presented workshops in which I have played the role of editor, coach, or director. But the influence has always gone both ways. As a researcher, I have studied in their classrooms, trusted their fieldnotes, synthesized their interpretations; I have learned about WritingLands by watching and sharing with them.

These research-wise teachers are acknowledged in the Appendix to this book. I especially thank the twelve original members of the 1984–85 research team who integrated computers into their writing workshops: Georgia Archibald, Gloria Casey, Jacqueline Collier, Marilyn Dell'Orco, Margaret Hasse, Brad Heger, Clara McCrary, Norma Owen, Peggy Ryan, Joan Krater Thomas, John Weiss, and Anne Wright. I also appreciate the administrators and teachers of the pilot schools (1985–87) where we developed the model of the Writing Improvement Team: Langston Middle School, Lindbergh High School, Steger Sixth Grade Center, and University City High School. Finally, I thank Joan Krater Thomas and the Webster Groves Action Research Team; since 1987 we have learned together how at-risk students can find their power as writers.

The Gateway Writing Project has received generous financial support, which has provided released time for me and assistantships for teachers who collaborated on the research. The Fund for Improvement of Postsecondary Education gave us a major three-year grant, which was enhanced by funding from the National Writing Project, the University of Missouri–St. Louis, and Harris-Stowe State College. My departments of English and educational studies juggled my teaching schedules to accommodate my field work, and the University of Missouri–St. Louis provided a semester's leave so that I could finish writing the book. Without such continuing support, this kind of longitudinal study would have been impossible.

I am intellectually indebted to three great teachers, James Britton,

Frank Smith, and Lou Smith, whose seminars introduced me to the processes of writing, reading, and qualitative research respectively. My dissertation committee at the University of Missouri–St. Louis coached me during the first years of the research: Wallace Ramsey, Richard Burnett, David Carkeet, Chris Madigan, Jon Marshall, and George McCall. Finally, Sallyanne Fitzgerald and Sally Barr Reagan read and responded to numerous drafts of these chapters in our monthly writing group.

My sons, Adam Pablo Flinn and Mark Hosteen Flinn, have grown up with this project. They began creating data when they wrote book reports, stories, and science projects on our home computers. They continue to support my writing time, to shield me from the telephone, and to prefer meals that we can microwave.

Welcome to WritingLand

Two twelve-year-old girls are working on "The Continuing Saga of Suzy Shell." They sit together at one microcomputer in their language arts classroom, holding the inspiration for their story—a seashell—as they talk and type their way through the plot:

> *Kathy:* "What should we do next?"
>
> *Betsy:* "Let's see [composing orally]. . . . Someone picks her up in the Caribbean Sea. . . ."
>
> *Kathy:* "No, that doesn't make sense."
>
> *Betsy:* "Well, we've got to get her out of there somehow."
>
> *Kathy:* [composing orally] "Cautiously Suzy came out of her shell. . . ."
>
> *Betsy:* "No, she can't come out, she'd get eaten!"
>
> *Kathy:* "Well, she could at least look. . . ."
>
> *Betsy:* "Okay, then [typing]. . . . *Suzy took a peek.* . . ."[1]

Although these writers were introduced to word processing just a few days ago, they are already using the computer to collaborate and to experiment with their writing. This vignette shows the promise: the active learning environment we call a "WritingLand." In a WritingLand workshop, students get support from a community of peers and teachers while they write by computer as well as by hand. But along with the promise, computers have brought new questions and new problems.

Asking the Right Questions about Computers and Writing

In the early 1980s, when I first learned of schools using computers to teach writing, I was cynical. As director of a National Writing Project site, I valued audience, voice, humor, conferences, a lively environment full of human sharing and communication. So the questions I muttered were mainly rhetorical: Are we now supposed to scrap our conferencing and interface with a machine? Are we going to isolate young writers in little study cubicles to be hooked on stimulus-response lessons and intergalactic graphics?

What I found, of course, was quite different. I learned that word processing is real writing and that the computer is a really wonderful writing tool. Like other teachers, I began planning my lessons on a word processor at home and reading student papers fresh from the printer. I began to visit classrooms in the St. Louis area, where several pioneering teachers were using computers in their writing workshops. I saw that the same machine which separated students in cubicles could bring them together in collaboration.

But I also saw that learning to teach well with computers brought a whole string of new and knotty practical questions. If my class has access only on Fridays to a computer lab at the far end of the school, what happens to the flow of a writing lesson and the rhythm of each student's writing process? If students catch the bus after school and cannot use computers at home, when do they get the uninterrupted time to draft and revise? If computers sit in straight rows jammed tight together, where do our writers spread out drafts and meet with peers? And how do I move around to hold conferences in such a lab without tripping over the cables? Teachers struggled with such problems and grumbled that the research was not written for process-oriented writing teachers.

What *does* the research say? When we look at the early studies of computers and learning, we see that researchers were asking quite different questions. Most saw word processing as an experimental "treatment" and asked what effect computers would have on student writing skills. Researchers designed experiments to test this question, only to find that the mere presence of computers does not do much to change revision, ideas, or overall quality (Collier 1983; Kane 1983; Withey 1983).[2] Others turned to individual case studies, asking how students revised with the computer. But they found that people used the new tools idiosyncratically, often to do more of the same things they did when writing by hand (Nichols 1986). They discovered that using a computer may enhance or even impede a writer's composing process (Bridwell, Sirc, and Brooke 1985).

A few results do appear fairly consistently. Studies show that most students enjoy writing at the computer; they collaborate willingly, write longer texts, and leave fewer mechanical errors. But if our question is, "Do computers improve writing?" the answer from research is inconclusive. Perhaps the questions are wrong.[3]

A growing body of knowledge, both from experiments and from case studies, sends one clear message to researchers: the computer is not a treatment, not a teacher, but a tool. Like the ballpoint pen, it is a writing tool that functions in a learning environment. Perhaps we need to ask less about tools, less about programs, and more about how to use them in specific classroom environments. Lucy Calkins explains, "The *content* of a writing lesson matters far less than the *context* of it" (1986, 12). We need to understand each context—its teaching, its social life, and its old and new writing tools. Only then can we hope to generalize about the role of computers in a writing community. As Gail Hawisher concludes in her 1989 review of forty-two research studies, we are "building a research base that relies less on a technocentric perspective than on a view informed by the interaction of technology with the culture in which it exists" (1989, 64).

Such an agenda seems to call for *action research* as a mode of inquiry.[4] Action researchers do their studies in real-world contexts. Instead of adopting a detached, experimental stance, they have a personal stake in the issues they are investigating. Usually, they work in teams that include both classroom practitioners and university consultants. What action research may lack in objectivity it gains in richness and practical use.

What We Asked and What We Learned

Since 1984, the Gateway Writing Project in St. Louis has been doing action research, much of it dealing with computers in the classroom. More than 150 experienced teachers have taken part in GWP's summer institutes on process approaches to teaching writing with computers. Dozens of our graduates have traced the progress of their own students in computer-equipped settings from grades 3 through college. Their schools represent diverse constituencies, ranging from the affluent suburbs to the urban core to the rural villages. The focus of our work has not been technology alone, but teachers, writers, and classrooms. We have asked what I believe is the big question: *How can we weave the computer into the human fabric of a writing workshop?*

In this book, I want to share what we have learned over the past five years. It is neither a research report nor a how-to manual. It is the story of committed teachers—writing specialists first, computer users second. I have watched them learning to integrate new electronic tools into their writing workshops. Together, as a research team, we studied what happened—the new energy, the new frustrations, the unplanned successes and the unplanned disasters. Our story suggests that what students do with any writing tool depends less on the power of the technology than on the power of the teacher.

Our teachers have designed classroom environments where computers enhance a process approach to teaching writing. You have already seen Kathy and Betsy at work in one of these settings. We call them "WritingLands"—analogous to the "Mathlands" proposed by Seymour Papert (1980) in *Mindstorms: Children, Computers, and Powerful Ideas*. A student of Piaget, Papert used computers to stimulate and support children in environments where they could manipulate objects, play with mathematical concepts, and feel pride in their own intelligence. Papert's Mathland reminds me of the sort of environment Britton (1970), Graves (1983), and Calkins (1986) suggest for writers: a place where children manipulate and play with language, where they feel pride in sharing and publishing their own work. I would like to define a *WritingLand* as a context that supports the learner through relationships with peers and teacher and through electronic as well as conventional writing tools.

What to Expect in This Book

To build a WritingLand, educators must take into account a whole range of contexts, from the individual writer to the classroom to the writing community in the school. The organization of this book follows the same sequence: as the story develops, its focus becomes wider and its questions, broader.

Part I looks closely at individual writers, asking "How can we describe the writing processes of students who use computers?" Part II looks at successful classrooms and their teachers, asking "Do computers promote any particular approach to writing?" and "How do process-trained teachers use the computer to foster good writing?" Part III maps out the features of a WritingLand community, asking, "How can we design computer-equipped environments that support students' growth in writing?" Part IV concludes by asking, "How can team leadership support teaching writing with computers throughout a school?" Part V describes our own experience with action research.

I've said that this book is neither a research report nor a how-to manual. Yet everything here is based on our research and also on our teachers' practical know-how. I want to make both the research and the know-how accessible to readers without breaking the flow of the story. You will find the research cited briefly in the text, with technical details in the chapter notes and particularly in chapter 20. You will also find specific ideas for teaching described throughout the text.

In this tour of WritingLands, sometimes we will survey a broad theme like the "writing process," showing the role it plays in actual classrooms. Sometimes we will zoom in for a close-up view of a single writer at work. At other times we will pause to observe a mini-lesson or to interview a teacher. By its very nature the story must be episodic and unfinished—it tells of new tools that are just beginning to affect writing in the schools. But by taking you on a tour of this half-charted territory, I hope to encourage you to explore further, to stake a claim, and to establish your own WritingLand.

Notes

1. Throughout this book, composing sessions and interviews are transcribed using the following conventions: All spoken language appears in quotation marks ("What can we write?"). All written text is italicized (*Suzy took a peek*). Written text read aloud has both italicization and quotation marks ("I like *took a peek*"). Comments on nonverbal behavior appear within brackets ("Cautiously Suzy came out of her shell" [composing orally]). When given, the names of the speakers appear italicized. These conventions do not apply to extracts presented in isolation during normal discussion.

2. Sarah Michaels (1986), reporting on the initially disappointing data from the Harvard Microcomputer and Literacy Project, concludes that the computer is not a treatment, not an independent variable that can be controlled and measured by the researcher. Instead, Michaels suggests that the computer is a "dependent variable": its impact is determined by other factors, such as teaching style, student writing activities, and classroom climate.

3. My discussion in this chapter is indebted to Gail Hawisher's lucid review of research in *Critical Perspectives on Computers and Composition Instruction* (Hawisher and Selfe 1989). She pulls together the findings of forty-two studies—twenty-six of them experimental, twelve case studies (including our Gateway Writing Project research), and four classroom ethnographies. Hawisher sees a growing consensus that we need to look beyond the computer as a single, definable "treatment." Instead, we should look at the introduction of computers as a contextual change, one that alters the learning environment in subtle ways (63–64).

4. My understanding of action research stems from a graduate course in qualitative methods with Professor Lou Smith at Washington University. While I knew that the National Writing Project had been encouraging research by classroom teachers, I came to see this movement as part of a recognized genre of inquiry; action research was legitimate! Chapter 20 contains a fuller discussion of the logic and the research methods our team of teachers used to gather the data for this book.

WritingLands

I Portraits of Student Writers

1 Writers at Work

Larry peers from his monitor to his most recent printout. Sitting at an oversized computer desk, he deletes a few words, then checks the draft to consider his next penned-in revision, then types the new text. He is editing the final copy of an essay which has developed through drafts, conferences, peer response, and seven printings in the course of two weeks.

"Yeah, we'd write some and then we had our group get-together in between to talk about them," he tells me. When a classmate handed back his paper, Larry would read over the comments and ask some questions. "Then we'd go back to the computer and decide if we want to use their suggestions. It's up to us—Mrs. Wright doesn't pressure us."

Twenty workstations like Larry's jut out from the walls of the writing lab at Hazelwood West High School, and at each, one of Anne Wright's seniors is working on some phase of the writing process. The boy next to Larry types directly from a handwritten draft. He explains, "I wrote one paper already, but I didn't like it so I started over."

Tamika is working to find a consistent tone in her comic impression of the school bus which brings her to this suburban high school from the city of St. Louis. "I stepped aboard the battlefield with caution," begins her draft, which leads into a portrait of "Dragonlady," the bus driver. Now she plans to extend her metaphor to describe a new freshman and the bully she defeats on her first day, armed only with a tuna fish sandwich. Tamika thinks about "victim," "prey," "culprit," and "villain," their connotations and images. She consults a teacher and a dictionary, and then tries out different versions by reciting them softly to herself. Pointing to her folder with five marked-up printouts and three sets of peer-response guides, Tamika smiles: "Mrs. Wright puts us through a lot of processes."

Any teacher who knows a good writing workshop will recognize what writers are doing in a computer-equipped WritingLand. They begin with group brainstorming or a mini-lesson and various individual planning techniques. They are guided to develop their papers through a series of drafts, meetings with peers, and conferences with the teacher. Their best work is carefully edited until the finished product can be presented to an audience—whether on the bulletin board, through the mail, or in a magazine.

The presence of computers makes some of these processes more challenging for teachers to manage, but it also enhances and motivates writing. Freed by the computer from recopying, most student writers are more willing to stick with the process until they have a publishable finished product. Larry and Tamika may sound like the fortunate few— college-bound seniors with access to a state-of-the-art lab. But we have found that a WritingLand can be created for students at any level and in any community.

Watch the writers in a much less elegant setting. Two groups of ninth graders are sharing a lab where they sit, elbow-to-elbow, reviewing their papers. The lab was built by removing a wall between a classroom and the library and by adding twenty-four computers.

Bev Hopkins's students are finishing the stories they have written and illustrated for publication. They have worked as editorial teams, marking one another's texts with symbols from a style sheet. Now the writers must review their printouts to make final changes on screen. Their teacher and three official peer tutors are available for help. Meanwhile the resource center teacher checks out software as well as books.

Sam calls for Bev Hopkins, pointing to one of the editorial marks on "The Transylvania Express," his soon-to-be-illustrated book.

"What does this mean?" asks Sam.

"What does your style sheet say?" Sam pulls out the sheet and she points to a rule for punctuation. He nods, reaches for the arrow keys, and inserts the missing comma.

In the same lab, Bruce Hanan's students are reviewing their essays for organization. They have already gotten comments from their teacher and peers, but today they are checking their essays again with a simple outlining program. The software was actually designed to support planning: a writer fills in the outline headings, then generates examples and explanations (a function with doubtful value except for writers who already know how to organize). Instead, Hanan uses the software to make students visually aware of structural problems. He asks them to read over their printouts and to create an outline matching their own intended plan of organization.

Ted looks skyward in dismay as he shows me his work-in-progress: "Now we've got to pull *that* [pointing to the outline on the screen] out of *this* [clutching his printed draft]. And we realize what we did wrong because you just CAN'T pull *that* out of *this!*" His insight comes less from the software than from Hanan's creative application of it. With good planning and some computer access, a WritingLand can develop from any process-oriented writing program.

A WritingLand can also be designed to support the learner with special needs. Gifted writers need a context for experimenting with arrangement, style, voice—for pursuing an idea at a level that challenges their own ability.

In Joan Krater Thomas's eighth-grade class, Youssef is proud to share his portfolio, especially his nine-page persuasive essay on the environment. The neatly typed paper has an unusual organization. Two fictional scenarios offer an optimistic and a pessimistic view of life in the next century, followed by a call for action to quell the greenhouse effect and other environmental hazards. Here is how Scenario 1 begins:

> "Beeeeep! Beeep!" The shrill ring of the alarm clock woke Henry from his dreams. Grumbling, he pushed himself out of bed and hustled to the bathroom. A motion detector above his head clicked and the bathroom lights came on.
>
> He entered the bathtub and turned the faucet. A measured amount of crystal-clear, solar-heated water shot out of the shower head. Clean water was in plentiful supply, thanks to a newly discovered method of inexpensively removing salt from sea water. But as a conservation measure, when five minutes of morning shower water were up, this water ceased to flow. . . .

Youssef explains that he began this essay with the idea of the scenarios. He drafted both of them by hand, then realized that he would need some kind of transition and some guidance for the reader. So at the computer, he laid out a plan:

Scenario 1—notebook
Bridge—copy 1
Scenario 2—notebook
Main Essay—copy 2

Once he found his organization, he used the computer to draft the transitional "bridge" and the main essay. Then he typed up the two scenarios and polished all four pieces at the keyboard until he was satisfied with the flow. From there, the paper developed easily. Youssef explains, "You can't get any sense of the flow unless you first have a picture of the whole."

In Joan Thomas's class, Youssef's writing has not been forced into prefabricated forms; he is accustomed to thinking through an organization to fit his own purpose, his own sense of the whole. Once finished, his essay is published in a typed and illustrated class collection between laminated covers. It's true that Youssef is a student who would do impressive work with any writing tool. But his writing-centered class and flexible software provide added support as he learns to manage the composing process with new authority.

Much as the computer appeals to gifted students, the ones who gain most from a WritingLand environment may be those labeled "basic" or "low-skilled" writers. The constant access to feedback and the frequent access to computers help them to make real progress with less frustration. Listen as Lori Brandman conferences with Carrie. The fifth grader is reviewing her paper about ice skating. Carrie has red-marked several spelling errors, added a few clarifying phrases, and elaborately crosshatched seven lines about other hobbies.

"Why?" asks her teacher.

"They don't have anything to do with ice skating," replies Carrie. With a smile of agreement, Brandman reads through the revised draft:

> I can do lots of tricks but not very good. They are turns, skids, trots, and sprays. My mom is teaching me a lot more about ice skating.
>
> And maybe I'll learn a lot more. . . . At my age is a good way to learn to iceskate. Why because sometimes your feet will hurt and complain and not want to get off.

At this point, her teacher intervenes, not to correct or criticize, but to ask for clarification:

> *Brandman:* "That's where I get mixed up, Carrie. Do you mean that you're at a particularly good age to be in training for ice skating?"
> *Carrie:* "If you're younger, your feet won't stop hurting and you'll be complaining."
> *Brandman:* "So your feet are developed enough now?"
> *Carrie:* "Yes, there's a book. . . ."

Suddenly, Carrie is the expert, telling her teacher something she didn't know. In this environment, Carrie learns that she has ideas worth reading and that she can talk her way into a passage when her written language falters. She finishes her conference and walks briskly to the computer room to do her final copy. Now that she has a focus and a voice, she knows she can produce a competent piece of writing.

A WritingLand workshop can succeed even with primary school children. Clara McCrary asks her third graders, "Do you know how to follow directions?" "Did you ever decide not to follow them?" "What happened?" The children discuss the consequences, sometimes funny, sometimes frightening, and then write quickly in their journals. Soon, most have drafted a short personal narrative.

"Who wants to read to us?" All around the room, hands go up. Myron walks to the front of the class, paper in hand. He stands tall as he shares his retelling of the time he played with matches and caught his shirt on fire. Twenty-five classmates listen attentively, then applaud.

Next Tammy comes forward to read her story about getting separated from her family at an amusement park: "I felt scared and lost—and then they found me."

Maurice reads just a sketchy report of an incident. His teacher prompts, "So what happened? What were the consequences?" He has no trouble explaining orally. "Okay, then. Write that down and finish it!" With a grin, he hurries back to his seat, grabs a pencil, and adds his new ending.

A day after this drafting session, McCrary will bring her class to the lab to type a revision on the computers. During a third session, she will help them proofread for spelling and mechanics, and finally they will enter corrections in the lab.

A WritingLand should not be seen as an educational resort for children from the affluent suburbs. Through daily experience with drafting, conferencing, and revising at the computer, children in urban environments internalize the writing process just as quickly.

Carol Henderson teaches third, fourth, and fifth graders in a turn-of-the-century school serving a rundown neighborhood in north St. Louis. Listen as two of her children tell a visitor from the university how they compose a paper:

> "First we write it on the computer. And then we talk to somebody about how they like the story and how to make it better."

> "Then Mrs. Henderson, she tell us what else we should do and we put in the disk and fix it some more."

> "Yeah, you keep on revising, and then you publish it. 'Cause you know for me, that's the bottom line—*publishing.*"

The three chapters which follow will take a closer look at a single WritingLand classroom and the students who learn there.

2 A Room Full of Writers

Peggy Ryan's language arts classroom is a deceptively simple WritingLand. Her sixth graders work with a modest stock of old and new writing tools in an environment that teachers can design without access to a lab or expensive equipment (fig. 1).

Two Apple IIe computers and a dot-matrix printer sit on a long table against the front blackboard. Small teacher-made posters hang above them, listing word-processing commands and symbols. Along the side window, a large rack offers *National Geographic World, 1-2-3 Contact,* and such computer magazines as *K-Power Enter.* Low bookcases of encyclopedias and dictionaries form a backdrop for a rotating rack of paperbacks, and two tall bookcases border a rug defining a quiet spot for reading or sharing writing. Chair-desks sit in rows but are often turned to form pairs and groups. A record player, tape recorder, and two old, manual typewriters (used when the computers are occupied) share a table in the rear. Bulletin boards display stories, poems, scripts, and reports—some handwritten, some printed, many illustrated.

In this environment, the computer doesn't stand out like a shiny chrome table in a room full of Early American. It just seems to belong, like a new species of fern in a room already flourishing with greenery. Computers also complement this teacher's design for instruction: the open classroom with a variety of learning centers. The front table serves as a writing center, just as the rug between the bookcases is a reading and response center.

This environment grew naturally from Peggy Ryan's experiences. An early participant in the Gateway Writing Project, she was already using a process approach to writing when she discovered computers. She had taken a short computer literacy course and enjoyed using other audiovisual equipment, so she quickly saw the potential of word processing. When the first two computers reached her school, she asked to try them for writing in her own classroom. A year later, I was fortunate to spend several hours each week for nine months as a guest in the WritingLand she was creating.

On the first day of school, when the temperature happened to be

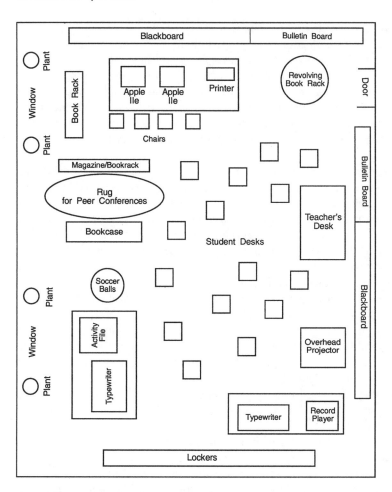

Fig. 1. Peggy Ryan's WritingLand classroom.

107°F, the sixth graders took turns entering captions and sentences at the keyboard. First they typed journal entries on the word *hot*; then they were each given an ice cube and asked to freewrite on *cold*. Ryan recorded in her log:

> Each student worked 10 minutes on computer writing about how they felt coming back to school in the extreme heat. A few needed a couple more minutes, one finished in 8 minutes, and one (new this year) refused to work on the computer. I think she was frustrated by her mistakes.

During the second week the computers were integrated into a series of activities about sea life. The teacher gave the writers one shell each from her own collection and guided them as they explored the shell with their five senses. Then she suggested they take notes on the animal who lived in the shell, directing them to reference books and nature magazines for more information. The writers composed by hand in their journals and waited their turns to type a revision at the computers. When two students finished writing, they would pair up, move their desks face to face, and read their drafts for the partner's response.

The next day brought a film and a discussion about specific sea creatures. Children were asked to close their eyes and imagine themselves as one of the creatures they had seen. A record of ocean waves played in the background as the writers got into the personae of their sea animals. This time a boy and a girl were invited to start composing directly at the keyboard while the others drafted in their journals.

All of the early assignments at the computer were brief creative pieces, usually descriptive paragraphs or short poems. The writers began with pieces that required minimal keyboarding but much revision, so they moved quickly beyond computer literacy into real composing. (Starting with a paper several pages long can frustrate even capable high school writers, who may get stuck in the learning bottleneck of slow typing.) By experimenting and playing with short texts, students came to see the computer as more than a fancy typewriter. The shell papers provided this kind of first experience for the fifteen sixth graders who spent about eight hours each week with Peggy Ryan.

Now let's take a closer look at this WritingLand. Five children sit in a book-sharing circle. Their teacher coaches them to "sell" their books by reporting the episodes that would interest their audience. She joins in discussing Laurie's novel, comparing the misadventure of her genie to the familiar tale of King Midas. At the same time, at the front of the room, Carol drafts at one computer and Ken revises a text at the other. Amy has printed out a long story and works alone at her desk to proofread. Back at the typewriter table, four boys work in pairs, dictionaries open, to revise a super-hero tale. Two others sit on the rug between the bookcases, sharing peer response, with occasional reference to the thesaurus; they read aloud, discuss their drafts, then record their revisions in pen on printout. Three girls work together on a vocabulary assignment. Some of their chatter is off-task, but the voices are low. As usual, the atmosphere is calm, orderly, pleasant, without tension. Children may ask a question of their teacher, but they don't pester her or depend on her for constant direction. They have learned to manage their own talking, reading, and writing processes in Peggy Ryan's class.

These were not specially selected children in a gifted program or a prep school. They attended a small parochial school in a middle-income neighborhood of blue-collar and office workers. (The small class of fifteen sixth graders was a fluke of declining enrollment; most grades had twenty or more.) Few of their parents had attended college, and the children spanned the full range of academic ability.

In this WritingLand environment, most students quickly gained confidence and fluency. By mid-fall, they were composing texts at the keyboard which were several pages long, such as dialogues and ghost stories to read to the primary classes. Often two writers would collaborate, taking turns as "typist" and as "thinkist" (Sheingold, Hawkins, and Char 1984). Just before Halloween, I watched two girls talk and type and experiment as they dramatized a crazy monster:[1]

> *Mary:* "*It puuulled the canvas out of the ground!*" '[composing orally, animated grin]
>
> *Linda:* [types Mary's line, two or three fingers on each hand, fairly fast] "*with a loud click. . . .*"
>
> *Mary:* "*No. . . .*"
>
> *Linda:* "*They hear this loud. . . .*"
>
> *Mary:* "*No . . .*" [hits RETURN and TAB] "*Then from the forest came a loud screech. . . .*"
>
> *Linda:* [types Mary's line] "*He covered his ears. . . .*"
>
> *Mary:* "*Somehow have him run!*"
>
> *Linda:* [typing] "*He covered his ears in rage as it ran. . . .*" [They overhear two boys at the next computer debating a turn in their own plot. The girls toss in a suggestion and resume work on their monster.]
>
> *Mary:* "*Not even feeling. . . .*"

This kind of playful, social composing thrives in a WritingLand. Far from inhibiting the children, the computer seems to fuel their enthusiasm—although they invent and revise stories by hand as well. As Ryan reported in her log:

> Some students like to work directly on the computer if they are writing a long story—they revise as they write. However most of them like to write smaller assignments (like poems) on paper, make them perfect(?) and then put them in the computer. . . . As they do they notice changes they want to make.

By early October, when this log entry was written, the list of those who liked to compose directly on the computer included Amy, the girl who would not touch the keyboard the first week. Amy overcame her initial distrust, and as the months went on, she experimented with drafting, editing, collaborating, and publishing with the computer. On a spring day, as she struggled with a technical problem, I realized how far she had come. Watch.

Amy is creating a myth to explain the origin of the rainbow. She tells of two goddesses who were rivals for the most beautiful colors. Her story contains a letter from Hecate challenging Aphrodite to a test. Using the TAB key, Amy sets up the letter with a boxed format, then prints a test copy (she knows that her software does not show the exact layout on the screen). To her delight, the printout is just right:

> Aphrodite,
>
> If you dare you will challenge me in a contest. The contest will be: The Battle for Color. If you win you will stay Goddess of Beauty and Love.
>
> Hecate

The next day Amy decides to revise her letter by inserting *in the middle of the forest, at sunset.* How can she do it without messing up her format? Amy knows there is an easy solution—putting the whole letter in quotation marks as a little paragraph within her myth, in the same way as she has learned to handle dialogue. But she likes her boxed format, and she is no longer afraid of the computer. She plays with the spacing, then asks for my help, and both of us try out commands until the text prints out a version that satisfies her.

Like Amy, most of the students in this WritingLand learned to trust the computer as a writing tool. As they grew familiar with the keyboard, they began writing more ambitious pieces—stories with episodes and chapters, or projects like a newspaper from Mt. Olympus, complete with cosmic headlines, gossip, classifieds, and an advice column. They could seldom get access to the computer to write an entire piece from start to finish. Yet when we surveyed the class in March, thirteen of the sixteen children said they preferred to compose directly at the keyboard when they could. Most of them insisted on doing at least the final copy of all their papers on the computer and as many of their drafts as possible. Each writer would file a finished paper in a personal portfolio and store it on a personal file disk. This way they could reread the paper from time to time and revise it again.

All of Peggy Ryan's students learned to write with the computer. But I noticed a great deal of individual variation in the way they worked the machine into their own processes and rhythms of composing.

Dave writes his first drafts very slowly, getting a whole piece planned out in his head before setting words to paper. He usually marks few changes on his printout during a session with his peer partner. But going back to the computer, he will develop his work, add new material, and make corrections to produce a strong final draft.

Carol tends to write a discovery draft on the computer, without much written or oral planning, and to fix most surface errors in the process. Then, during peer response, she makes penciled notes on her printout. She revises this text at the computer, changing words, phrases, and whole sentences, and then goes on to add new text composed at the keyboard.

Gary and Ken don't usually revise their original texts very much. When they return to a story, they like to add more episodes. My field-notes describe them as fluent at the keyboard: "Ken types rapidly, thumb for space bar, no draft. . . . Looks mainly at screen. He plunks authoritatively."

Jim quickly types through a first draft, but he leaves so many errors and omissions that his text is hard to read. Toward the end of the school year, he writes a myth about "a great sculpture named Tiesas" and the jealous Ontilo—"the one how did the sculpting for the gods before Tiesas came along." Here is a passage from his first draft:

> When Tiesas was wresting Ontilo asked him if he would be famuos to millions of people. Tiesas was very excited he said yes. But then he asked "But how?" you will find out very soon.

During his peer meeting, Jim fixes many of the surface errors (*He was the one who did the sculpting . . .*) and develops the plot by adding detail and motivation. He goes back to the computer with a heavily marked-up printout. His revised passage becomes:

> So he went to the chamber where the God zeus help his lightning bolts. He looked around there was no one there. So he took some bolts and ran. when Tiesas was reasting when Ontilo asked him if he wanted to be known all over the world. Tiesas was thrilled , he said yes. But then Tiesas asked "But how?" you will find out very soon.

Although it still has many errors and confusing elements, Jim's revision is much improved. It also shows revision at all levels, for detail and organization as well as wording and mechanics.

Different writers, different composing processes, different ways of using writing tools. As we planned our action research, Peggy Ryan and I asked two of her sixth graders to serve as case study writers during the first year they worked with computers. The next two chapters will offer close-up views of these writers, one very talented and verbal ("Mary"), the other a reluctant writer with a history of school failure ("Bob").[2]

In November I met at the computer table with Mary and Bob to discuss their role in the research. By then I was no stranger. During my weekly visits, Mary had often talked with me about her writing. This time I explained what we were hoping to learn: "This is one of the first classes in St. Louis to have computers in the room every day, so your experience could really help us. One of the things we want to know is how students revise their papers, and I've seen that you do a lot of revising." Would she help? Her response was enthusiastic. She agreed to keep a log with records of her writing topics, the time she spent writing by hand and by computer, and any ideas she might want to share.

Seated quietly next to her, Bob was noncommittal. Since he surely knew that he was not one of the best writers in class, I tried to relieve his discomfort by talking directly about his selection. I pointed to one of his papers: "Bob, I've noticed you have a really strong natural voice, but you always spend a lot of time fixing your spelling. The computer might make editing easier for you. If we study your writing, I think we'll learn some things we can teach other kids next year. Will you help us?" Bob listened closely and agreed to help, but he didn't show Mary's exuberance. Only one aspect of the research made Bob grin— the big spiral log with *UM–St. Louis* stamped in gold. As the other boys rushed over to admire it, he carefully clipped it inside his three-ring binder and slipped his latest printout into the pocket. Our research partnership was now official.

Doing case studies is a wonderful way to learn how writers think and how they develop. But I found that doing case studies of writing with computers brings some new technological dilemmas. To understand a writer at work, I need to capture the whole composing process— including the false starts, the accidental deletes, and the pauses for rereading. With pen-and-paper composing, it is easy to preserve a paper record of the process. For example, I could simply ask Bob or Mary to save their drafts and make all changes with a single strikeover in contrasting ink. But with word processing, the text is just a pattern of lighted points until printed in hard copy. Any changes my writers made in process would vanish in electronic amnesia.

To get an accurate view of composing at the keyboard, I commissioned a new piece of software. Programmer John Oberschelp of Milliken Publishing Company in St. Louis designed an enhancement to his Milliken Word Processor.[3] COMPTRACE records every keystroke as a writer composes, and then replays the composing session on the monitor as the writer is interviewed.

Children usually have a hard time recalling and explaining to a researcher how they wrote a particular piece. But with COMPTRACE, Bob and Mary were able to produce a vivid picture of their writing decisions. Many of their comments quoted in the next chapters were elicited by showing the "instant replays" and asking, "What were you trying to do when you made these changes in your story?"

These case study writers collaborated with us in research on their own learning processes. Scardamalia and Bereiter (1983) call their subjects "coinvestigators"; Mohr (1984) calls them "coauthors." Bob and Mary certainly filled both roles in the action research on which this book is based.

Notes

1. Remember the conventions used for portraying student work that were mentioned in "Welcome to Writingland," note 1.

2. For the complete case study portraits of Bob and Mary, see chapter 5 of Flinn 1986a.

3. COMPTRACE is based on a program developed at the University of Minnesota for research with adult writers (Bridwell, Sirc, and Brooke 1985). Lillian Bridwell demonstrated this software at a conference in 1985 and encouraged me to design something along the same lines that might work for young children. COMPTRACE was developed for the Milliken Word Processor, which is easy, menu-driven, and low in memory requirements.

Since COMPTRACE is not a free-standing program, it will not record for other word processors. But with the help of John Oberschelp, I have explained the method for programming such keystroke recording software and also some alternative ways to videotape the composing process (Flinn 1987a).

3 Mary

Portrait of a Skillful Writer

On the September day when Peggy Ryan handed out her shell collection, Mary was introduced to the tiger cowrie—and to the computer. She examined the shell, using her five senses. She read about its former resident and penned a paragraph-long description in her journal. Rereading her draft, she marked a few changes with arrows. Then she entered this ninety-five-word text at the computer:

> THE TIGER COWRIE HAS AN ORANGISH STRIPE AND BLACK DOTS WITH LIGHT BLUE SHADOWS ON ITS BACK. IT LOOKS AS IF A GREAT ARTIST PAINTED IT PERFECTLY, THEN SOMEONE PICKED IT AND PUT A THIN SHEET OF GLASS OVER ITS SMOOTH TEXTURE. ON ITS OTHER SIDE IT HAS A OPENING WITH FIERCE TEETH GROWLING AT YOU.IF YOU PUT IT UP TO YOUR EAR YOU CAN HEAR THE SOFT WHISPER OF THE OCEAN BUT UNDER ALL OF ITS BEAUTY IT IS JUST A SMALL TOY BEATIFULLY CONSTRUCTED BY NATURE.FOR THE OCEAN TO PLAY WITH.

Comparing the draft in Mary's journal with her printed revision shows that, for the most part, she simply recopied this description. But already she was aware that she could critique her text and change it as she typed. The last line of her handwritten draft simply read: *Under all of its beauty it is just a small shell . . . for the ocean to play with.* She substituted *toy* for *shell* as she typed, creating a lovely extended metaphor.

More than most sixth graders, Mary was prepared to use the computer as a writing tool. She already revised willingly with pen and paper. Although she had no training on the keyboard, she had used a neighbor's electric typewriter a few times. A bright, verbal, eleven-year-old, Mary was doing well in all her classes. Her scores on writing samples and standardized tests placed her near the top of her age group.[1] Mary adjusted to word processing as easily as she did to most school activities.

Through a year of visits and interviews, I learned from Mary how one capable student can weave the computer into her own writing process. She talked freely about her writing and her reading. She saved and reviewed drafting sessions with COMPTRACE, tape-recorded her meetings with peer partners, and sat with me, during class and during recess, to discuss how her writing was going. Often she brought me drafts of stories in process. What she shared creates a picture of an adolescent who has become literate.

Mary reads a great deal. She especially likes mysteries and books where "a lot of good things and a lot of bad things happen." She often reads at her desk, sometimes sprawled in a chair with a blanket around her. Mary also likes to write. She speaks proudly of her self-sponsored writing, which includes "pretty many stories and some poems." She keeps her work in "a special desk drawer." She also expresses pride in the special portfolio and file disk that are stored in class with her name on them. It seems that the distinction becomes blurred between self-sponsored writing and school-sponsored writing because, in her classroom, students choose many of their own topics and develop their papers at their own pace.

In her log, Mary describes herself as *a fairly good writer. . . . What I like about my writing is how it slowly flows together. . . . But what I don't like is that most of the time I can't stop it from being so boring and it goes on forever.* Her strongest point as a writer, she explains, is *description.* She finds the computer an asset: *I don't have to worry about doing 2 or 3 drafts I just use the cursor and go over it.* Mary's self-assessment highlights two points common to many capable student writers: she composes fluently and she is willing to revise repeatedly. It also cites some of her personal concerns.

"Do you like to start your papers at the computer?" I ask after she has used word processing for several weeks. "Or would you rather draft first by hand?" Mary explains that she often starts in her journal and then copies the text at the keyboard, making some changes in her head. But she prefers to compose directly at the computer: "When I'm typing it out I have more time to think—I'm looking at the keys and thinking about the story." (Just copying on the computer is "boring.")

When Mary wants to revise she meets with her writing partner to mark changes with pen on printout: "I read out loud to Linda, and if there's a part that doesn't sound good she'll say, 'Add something there.'" The suggestions most often involve making the text more detailed and "more descriptive," a quality both Mary and Linda prize. After marking her revisions on the hard copy, she enters them at the computer.

Mary's Writing Process

In November, Peggy Ryan gave her class a newspaper clipping about a ten-year-old boy who caught a burglar. The students were asked to write a narrative from one character's point of view.

"Can it be a girl?" Mary asked in a prewriting discussion.

"No, it's got to be a boy!" retorted a male classmate.

"You want to be the heroine of this story?" Their teacher agreed that would be fine, and Mary set to work.

By observing how she develops her news story, we can gain a closeup view of the composing process of a talented young writer. I will make special note of how and what Mary revises. These revising decisions will show her emerging taste, her sense of what "good writing" is. They will also show how she uses the computer to achieve her own writing goals.

I watched from the side of the room as Mary began drafting her news story at the keyboard. She brought no notes. Eyes focused on the monitor, she typed quite fluently, rarely stopping to hunt for a key and using two, three, or four fingers. She let the computer wrap words and begin new lines, reserving the carriage return for ending paragraphs. Often she fixed typos in process by deleting back to an error and retyping whole words; sometimes she even added whole sections in this inefficient way—deleting words, adding new text, then retyping what she had deleted. At other times, though, she deftly used the cursor to return to the spot and insert her addition. After three months of regular work with a new writing tool, Mary's keyboarding skills, though primitive, did not interfere with her composing.

One reason the computer didn't slow her down is that Mary's natural composing rhythm was not based on fast, fluent discovery-drafting. Throughout her news story, she worked consciously on style as well as plot. She kept revising her first sentence until she was satisfied. Starting with *Who*, she paused, fussed with punctuation, deleted it, then typed *I felt very scared at first*, paused, then deleted the whole lead and typed *I heard a knocking at the door*.

The rest of Mary's first draft flowed rather quickly, with only minor, mainly surface, changes in process. After completing her story, she moved back to the start to reread, adding an omitted period and repairing a slightly garbled sentence. At the end of her thirty-minute first session, she printed out this 197-word draft (she had accidentally begun with the caps lock on):

> I HEARD A KNOCKING AT THE DOOR. MY MOTHER AND
> FATHER HAD TOLD ME NOT told not to answer it no matter

what so I didn't. Then I went into my room and started playing. When my dog came in and dove under the bed I thought it was strange but when I heard the glass break I grabbed the phone and did the same.I didn't look out at all.I just dialed 911 and started telling them what had happened.

By the time they got here the robber was out in the hall searching.When he heard the sirens he ran franticlly into my closet.I was going to lock him in but then the police burst through the door.I was just to shocked to tell them where thomas was much less say anything else.

When they finally found him I got up and they took me outside.At that point I didn't want to talk to the reporters I just wanted to see my mom and dad.

When they got back I ran over to them and gave them a big hug. After a while I decided to talk to the reporters.

The next day Mary met with Linda, her writing partner, for thirty minutes. During this session she penned revisions directly on her printout, changing virtually every sentence (fig. 2). Later, Mary and I used COMPTRACE to replay a portion of her first composing session. We also examined the marked printout from her peer-response meeting. Then she explained how she had gone about developing her story.

When Mary reread her first draft, she said she didn't like it much. With Linda's help, she tried to "make it sound better so the words and paragraphs kind of tell about the same thing." She didn't want it to "skip over like from when the robber ran in until I was calling the police, so I made something in between." She added a first paragraph telling "when" and "where" the story took place—Ryan's assignment had specified the "5 W's." She changed *knocking* to *rapping* because it "sounded more descriptive, like if you were using 'walking' and changed it to 'strolling.' " (" 'Knocking,' " she explained, "is used all the time, like 'walking.' ") Mary also felt the whole piece was getting "kind of long" and some parts needed to be cut. "The dog didn't fit into the story," so, with the ruthlessness of an adult editor, she got rid of him.

The next day, Mary spent another thirty minutes retyping at the computer. I watched her begin with the new lead, letting the old text slide ahead of it. Then she started fixing her story, a paragraph at a time. Here is her final, 247-word story:

It was 6:00 in the evening.I was in my room listening to my radio and doing my homework.My dad had gone deer hunting and my mom was at the store.

I heard a rapping at the door.I had to finish a sentence and by the time I got to the door whoever had been there was gone.So I went into my room.

All of the sudden I heard a loud crash.I was going to see what it was but then I heard the banging footsteps.I grabbed my phone and hid under the bed.I didn't look out at all.I just called the police and started telling them what had happened.Then I hung up.

After that I heard my door open and I froze stiff.Whoever was out there ran frantically when he heard the sirens.The police burst through the door and I slowly got up.

They pulled the robber out of the closet and I nearly fainted knowing that he had hidden in the closet right next to me and I didn't even know.

They carefully took me outside.At that point I was to frightened to talk to anyone.I just walked up to the nearest policeman and asked him to get my mom and dad.

My dad couldn't come but when my mom finally came I ran over to her and gave her a big hug.Then I told her and the reporters what had happened.

Though most of Mary's final draft consisted of recopying her penned-in changes, she also revised while typing. Several times she substituted whole phrases or clauses to produce a more mature style. For example, during the peer-response meeting she had added, *They pulled him out of the closet and roughly arrested him*; at the keyboard, this sentence became, *They pulled the robber out of the closet and I nearly fainted knowing that he had hidden in the closet right next to me and I didn't even know*. When I asked her about this revision, Mary explained, "It shows my character's feelings more; the other way it was looking just at the burglar." Her last sentence was also rewritten. A penned-in revision, *Then I told her everything that had happened and I also told the reporters*, became more concise: *Then I told her and the reporters what had happened*. I don't feel that all of Mary's changes improved her story. Yet, on the whole, the final paper is more vivid and coherent than her draft, two of the qualities she had cited as goals.

Consider what this news story has shown about Mary's composing process. We see a great deal of revision at all levels, with a willingness to scrap whole sentences and paragraphs. Mary works with larger units of text (phrases, clauses, and sentences), a pattern researchers have observed among skillful, mature writers.[2] While she makes many typographical and mechanical errors, she corrects most, either in process, as she notices them, or with her peer partner in a later proofreading check.

Mary talks about her writing with a rich awareness of her own goals and performance. Instead of justifying her decisions with textbook rules, she tends to use rhetorical explanations. For example, she comments on the news story in terms of voice (show the character's

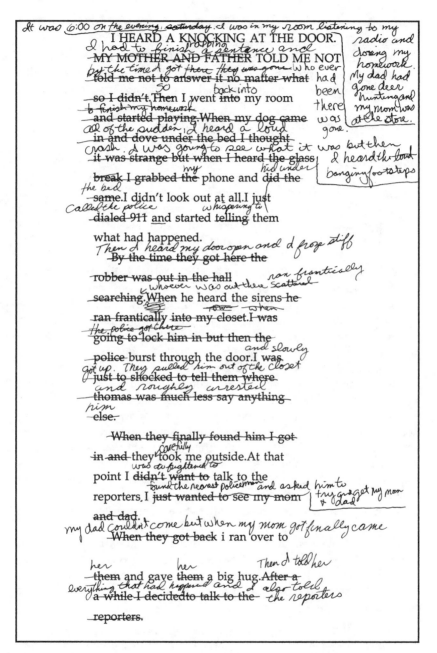

Fig. 2. Mary's revisions marked during peer conference.

feelings by adding "I nearly fainted"), audience (the story shouldn't skip around), or purpose (delete the dog).

She learned this mode of discourse naturally in her WritingLand community. As a process-oriented teacher, Peggy Ryan usually talks in just this way about student as well as professional writing.

The Process in a WritingLand Community

At one time I thought I understood *the* writing process. Watching these children convinces me that there are as many versions of the writing process as there are writers. At one time I assumed that the computer would lend itself to certain kinds of composing, that there might even be a "computer composing process." But watching Mary and my other case study writers convinces me that the computer is a flexible writing tool, transparent to whatever process the writer may use.

We might say that one mark of a skillful writer is the ability to vary the composing process for specific purposes—jotting quickly in a journal, editing carefully to publish. Another mark is the ability to use feedback to improve a paper. (A powerful revising tool is not much use to a writer who cannot see anything to improve.) Finally, skilled writers can take advantage of different tools for different purposes at different points in the composing process. Let's watch Mary.

In the news story, her process went something like this: *teacher input → discussion → computer draft → peer response → computer draft → conference.* Most of her major class papers follow a similar process, sometimes beginning with a pencil draft, sometimes at the computer. Often there are additional computer drafts alternating with peer response or conferencing. After watching her develop a number of papers, I began to understand how she works. I saw that no matter how extended or quick her composing process, the bulk of Mary's revising happens when she meets with her peer partner. The WritingLand community is really the power that drives her composing process.

This power is clear in the development of Mary's most ambitious story, "Pot Belly Bear." The first pencil draft covered seven pages. After she talked it through with Linda, the paper had so many erasures, arrows, inserts, and cross-outs that it was almost indecipherable. Here is the opening paragraph:

> We love the pot belly bear, the pot belly bear. Su-ure they all love the Pot Belly Bear. But "here I am still in the department store all by my self," mumbled Pot Belly Bear. . . . "Out of all these shoppers there has to be somebody who'd love and want just me. I'm loveable and squeezable and looking for a friend.

Although the idea is not original, this bear already has a distinct and appealing voice. Mary read the draft aloud in class, at the urging of classmates who wanted me to hear it. She explained that she was struggling with point of view. How could she make Pot Belly Bear tell his own story and also include descriptions from the outside? On the pencil draft she experimented by erasing "I" in favor of "He" and changing some direct quotations to indirect ones. At the computer she again tried, then rejected, a third-person narrator. In her log she explained that she had a problem *seperating what I think and what I say. But I think it is going to turn out good.* "Pot Belly Bear" did turn out "good," but only after several more conferences and revisions at the computer.

From the start, writing this paper was a social act, one which was responded to by many audiences: peer partner, whole class, teacher, researcher. The feedback from this writing community helped Mary stick with "Pot Belly Bear" through weeks of revision.

Mary liked to mull over her papers. Yet at times she used quite a different, truncated process. As an example, we'll look at how she wrote a brief sketch of a chipmunk—no feedback, little revision. Her teacher had suggested to several writers that they choose a magazine picture and then brainstorm a list of alliterative descriptions. Figure 3 shows what Mary penned in her journal. At the computer she composed this final portrait:

> Crouched on colorful, crisp leaves
> the curious but cautious chipmunk
> closely listens for danger. As it moves
> along its way the cheeky chipper
> pauses, flicks its tail, and calls a
> chip-chip-chirrup.

Mary especially liked this piece because it "just came right out" and needed no further revision. The computer produced a neat-looking copy, but in this case it was really used as a typewriter. Mary revised in her head when entering text, shaping her language "at the point of utterance" (Britton et al. 1975, 26). The process went like this: *teacher input → brainstorming by hand → drafting by computer.*

I've said that Mary—like most student writers—makes dramatic changes in a paper only when she gets response. Let's take a closer look at the peer meetings in her WritingLand, where most decisions on substantive revision are made. In the example which follows, Mary is acting as critic rather than as author.

Linda has drafted a science fiction story at the computer, made a printout, and brought it to her desk to share with Mary. (The process

is *computer drafting* → *peer response with pen* → *computer drafting*.)
Here is the opening paragraph of Linda's draft about a girl who
discovers that her home is on a distant planet:

> Allison thought she was a normal girl with a normal family until
> now. Her parents died in a car accident when she was twelve
> years old. that was three years ago and she was living with her
> aunt.

This story is typical of the fiction written by young adolescents. The
plot is contrived, the characters thin, and the theme totally free of
deeper meanings. It's imaginative play. Graves (1983) and Calkins
(1986) reject such fanciful stuff and tend to guide even young children
toward informative and personal writing. But as Myra Barrs explains
(1983), Britton and his English followers see this as a healthy stage in
development, one that will gradually yield to more mature literary
and psychological awareness. Peggy Ryan favors the British view, and
allows her students to find their own paths into fiction.

When Linda and Mary met to review this story, they continued the
composing process orally. Their dialogue, which we taped, is a record
of thinking and problem-solving:

> *Mary:* "I think the normal girl with a normal family sounds kind
> of. . . ."
>
> *Linda:* "Yeah, it does. Oh . . . go get the thesaurus! What should
> we look up? We could put. . . ."
>
> *Mary:* "Wait, just take off . . . 'Allison thought that she . . . and her
> family . . . were normal.' I don't know, that doesn't sound good."
>
> *Linda:* "Well, if you're on Earth you would think you're born
> there."
>
> *Mary:* "Well, from what I understand, she was born here, but her
> grandparents and her mom were from the planet Zagar? 'Allison
> thought . . . she was just like any other girl until now.' "
>
> *Linda:* "That sounds good. . . . Noooo—'Alison thought she was
> just like any other girl until her parents died in a car accident.'
> I think *that* is good!" [reads line again]
>
> *Mary:* "Nooo . . . 'until her parents had a strange disappearance.' "
>
> *Linda:* "No . . . 'Allison thought she was just like any other girl
> until one day her parents mysteriously disappeared.' " [They
> both smile in agreement.]

These girls were accustomed to working as partners. Mary took
such an active role in this conference that her "feedback" might better
be called "collaborative revision." I watched many peer meetings in
this WritingLand which showed the same active, critical, yet playful,
engagement.

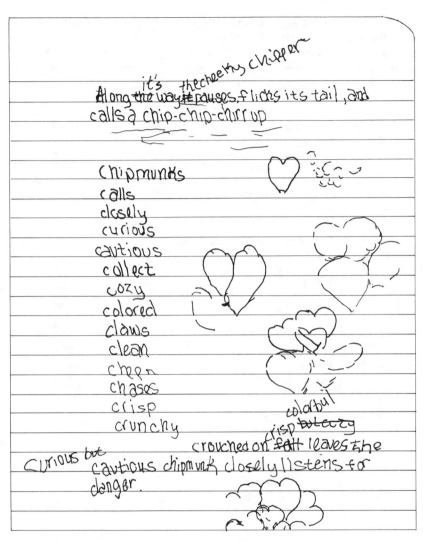

Along the way *it's the cheeky chipper* pauses, flicks its tail, and
calls a chip-chip-chirr up

Chipmunks
calls
closely
curious
cautious
collect
cozy
colored
claws
clean
cheen
chases
crisp
crunchy

colorful
crisp but crazy

Curious but cautious chipmunk closely listens for danger. crouched on fall leaves the

Fig. 3. Mary's prewriting: chipmunk description.

Along with revising together, Mary and Linda often talked their way through whole papers, sometimes by hand, sometimes side by side at the computer. Inspired by a picture of a sunset, they brainstormed the following sketch in a half hour at the keyboard, with Mary doing most of the typing:

Sunset 1

The trees sway in the gentle breeze as the ocean creeps up upon the horizon. The bushy clouds The sun peeks over its dreary kingdom. The shadows soon to fade reaching out to the mountains. The mountains slowly touch the sky. The birds will soon flutter over this tropical paridiese. All the beauty on this island is perfectly formed with natures soft hands.

Listen to some of the dialogue which created that piece:

Mary: "The trees rustling in the gentle breeze."

Linda: "The trees—something trees. . . ."

Mary: "Creepy—they look creepy."

Linda: "The driven—"

Mary: "No, don't put that. . . . [pauses, drums fingers]

Linda: "The bushy trees [pause] in the gentle breeze."

Mary: [Types] *"bushy trees"*

Linda: "Rustle."

Mary: [Types] *"sway in the gentle breeze"*

Mary: [Types] *"the ocean creeping up* upon the horizon."

Linda: "—Up upon the what?"

Mary: [Types] *"upon the horizon."*

Linda: "Then put. 'The something clouds hanging. . . .' "

Mary: "I know, let's write, 'The bushy clouds. . . .' " [They read through text on screen.]

Both: *"The trees swaying in the gentle breeze. The ocean creeps up on the horizon."*

Mary: "We've got to connect this. . . ."

Two weeks later the girls returned to the computer. Though Mary usually marked up her drafts during conferences, this time they marked no changes on their printout. The revision, like the original, grew through oral collaboration at the keyboard:

Sunset 1

The trees sway in the gentle breeze as the ocean creeps upon the horizon. Bushy clouds gently float above while the sun peeks over its dreary kingdom. The mountains reach towards the sky as their shadows are fading away. Flocks of birds will soon flutter over this tropical paradise. The wind briskly rustles through the island. The beauty of it was perfectly created by natures soft hands.

Mary was very pleased with this sketch—"You could just feel you were there, all relaxed." The process of writing "Sunset" can be mapped like this: *planning (oral), drafting, response—with partner at computer → response, redrafting—with partner at computer.*

Don Graves (1983) notes that when students choose their own topics, they often pursue one through several related papers. Later in February, Mary chose another sunset picture. But this time, she composed alone, and, without peer response, her process was strikingly different. Here is her first pencil draft:

Sunset 2

The sky fades into orangish colors as the sun slowly sets above the mountains. A soft line of clouds drifts peacefully under the sun. The trees are reaching higher and higher soon to reach their destination. The hill's green grass is gently waving in the smooth breezes. The sun looks down at the land as if to say good night before it disappears into the night. Soon it will all be shadows waving in the wind.

During the next few days she entered and revised her text at the computer. Here is the finished piece:

Sunset 2

The sky fades into orangish colors as the sun slowly sets above the mountains. A soft line of clouds drift peacefully under the sun. The trees are reaching higher and higher until they fianlly touch their destination. The hill's green grass is gently waving in the smooth breeze. The sun looks down at the land as if to say good-bye before it disappears into the night. Soon it will all be nothing but shadows waving in the wind.

Mary made two printouts, but in the second she revised just one detail—fixing a redundancy by changing *reach their destination* to *touch their destination*. (The extra "draft," printed after changing just one word, seems unique to computer revising; I never saw a student recopy an entire paragraph by hand in order to improve a single word.)

Watching Mary develop these two descriptions, I was struck by how much more experimentation and revision took place in the collaborative "Sunset 1." Like many bright middle school writers, Mary knows *how* to revise. But she knows *what* to revise only through the support of peer feedback, teacher conferencing, or collaboration which she gets from her WritingLand community. Alone, even with a powerful electronic revising tool, her process is truncated: *draft by hand → recopy by computer*. Revision for Mary is not yet fully internalized—it requires some external scaffolding.

Of course even experienced adults need response during the writing process. As I wrote this chapter, I found myself stuck in draft after draft that seemed to flounder. Meeting with my own peer group of writing teachers helped me find my organization and my focus. Peter Elbow (1973) says we can work alone, "growing" a paper, until our ideas run cold; then we need hot feedback from readers to go on "cooking" a paper until it's done. Rarely do any of us produce our best work in isolation, without feedback.

The difference between Mary and the unskilled writer is that she knows how to use feedback to revise and improve her drafts; often the unskilled writer has trouble applying feedback even when it is given. Because Mary works so well with response, it is startling to see how little she revises without it. In time, Mary will probably internalize the revision process more fully. She will notice on her own more of the changes she needs to make, and she will give herself the sort of feedback she so often hears in conferences. But, like most of us, she will probably still write better and revise more with response.

Table 1 shows how Mary's composing process varies depending on whether or not she gets feedback from an audience while she is writing. The pattern is consistent, regardless of her writing tools. A computer makes revision easy, but only a human audience makes it essential.

Good Writing Is Descriptive

I came to see that Mary's composing decisions were guided by an implicit sense of "good writing." While her taste was not always that of an adult critic, she knew what she liked, and she knew how to revise to reach her own goals. The sunset sketches provide a clue to Mary's personal model: *good writing is descriptive*. This model helped Mary to develop her papers with interesting details. At the same time, it often enticed her to add nice-sounding but rather empty adjectives. Look what happened to the brief sketch "Fall":

[draft]

Fall is plumb pumpkins, falling leaves, and crunching apples

[revision]

Fall is plump, juicy pumpkins, leaves falling from their branches, and sinking your teeth into a delicious, scarlet red apple.

[draft]
swift deer and squirrels with bushy tails

[revision]
swift deer and tiny little squirrels with long bushy tails

The new descriptions are longer but no more meaningful. And by adding adjectives to the lead, Mary lost her neat, parallel series. Months later, reviewing this piece in her portfolio, she noticed some surface errors but showed no dissatisfaction with such empty descriptors as *tiny little* or *scarlet red*.

Sometimes Mary moved beyond this kind of flowery revision. "Pot Belly Bear" was developed by tightening and sharpening, not just by adding adjectives. See how her first draft presents Pot Belly Bear's new owner:

> And before pot belly bear knew it he was being lifted up from his place and handed to the man.
> "You're just right, just perfect!" Said the man.
> Pot belly bear was so happy he gave the man a big hug and held on tightly to his arm he was even happier when he heard the man say. . . .
> "Never mind about the bag I'll just carry him" Said the man.
> "I know I'm going to like him. . . ."

Mary's final version is half the length and stronger:

> Before Pot Belly Bear knew it he was being lifted up and put into the mans arms.
> "Don't put him in a bag I'll just carry him," Said the man.
> "I know I'm going to like him. . . ."

Mary summed up her progress in a brief writing autobiography written near the end of the school year:

> My writing has changed much in the course of the year. It has gone from longer and less descriptive on the beginning of the year to snappier stories and poems with lots of description towards the end of the year. Now I enjoy just sitting down at the computer and quickly typing out easy, quick stories. I guess some of it is because I have become used to the keyboard and can type much faster.

Mary saw the computer as a tool for writing and an asset to her writing process. Yet her model of "good writing" led her to develop finished products that were uneven in quality. She could become enamored of pretty adjectives and flowing phrases just moments after crafting a well-honed line.

"The Myth of Rosarina," part of a class project on Greek myths,

Table 1
Response and Mary's Composing Processes

Response	Processes
Yes	
Pot Belly Bear	Pencil draft → peer response → computer draft → peer response → computer draft. . . .
Sunset 1	Plan, draft, response w. partner at computer → response, redraft with partner at computer
News story	Computer draft → peer response → computer draft → conference
Science fiction tale	Computer draft → peer response → computer draft → peer response → computer draft. . . .
No	
Chipmunk	Pencil brainstorming → computer draft
Sunset 2	Pencil draft → computer recopy
Cowrie shell	Pencil draft → computer recopy

has both kinds of revision. Sometimes Mary skillfully sharpens and clarifies:

[draft]

One day Athena the goddess of wisdom and handicrafts saw how beautiful Rosarina's works were and she knew that if Rosarina was not killed that soon she would be as good as Athena herself.

When asked what she thought of this passage, Mary described the sentence as too long with "too many 'ands.'" Also, she felt *as good as Athena* "could mean anything—I wanted to show she was good at making clothes!" So she revised accordingly:

[revision]

One day Athena the goddess of wisdom and handicrafts saw how beautiful Rosarina's works were. She knew that if Rosarina was not killed that soon she would make clothes as beautiful as Athena herself did.

Elsewhere in the story, Mary's revisions are less effective; she simply adds nice-sounding adjectives:

[draft]

Now Rosarina would brighten everyones day after it rains, and Aphrodite could see her daughter.

[revision]

Now Rosarina would brighten everyone's day after a horrible rain, and Aphrodite could again see her wonderful daughter, Rosarina.

Yet Mary knew what she was doing. She offered a very precise assessment of this text, based on her own goals for revision: "I like description. I added two more adjectives to make it more descriptive." Mary was working from a consistent personal model of good writing.

The computer provided support for Mary's goals. At the keyboard, she could play with adding and substituting details until she created a description she liked. Note that the computer itself did not lead her to a more sophisticated view of good writing. (Word processing can be used just as easily to prune or proofread as to describe, but Mary did not focus on these goals.) Instead, it seems that Mary integrated the computer into an already-familiar approach to the process. This is consistent with findings (Hawisher 1989) of case studies that involve older writers.

Someday, if Mary changes her model of good writing, it will probably come through teaching and maturing, not simply through new writing tools. The computer is "programmed" by the writing community. As Mary continues to get social support and feedback in her WritingLand classroom, she will probably start asking more of the computer.

Notes

1. The Gateway Writing Project's research team designed a writing sample to assess students in grades 3 through 12. Mary's paper, scored with sixth, seventh, and eighth graders, received a 9 on a 2–12 scale. Her California Achievement Test scores showed a National Percentile of 97 in Total Language, 92 in Total Reading.

2. Lillian Bridwell (1980) and Nancy Sommers (1980) found that skilled college and adult writers could manipulate larger units of text, while less-experienced students focused on surface revisions. Lucy Calkins (1980) observed a similar pattern among elementary school children, who initially identified revision with correcting spelling and capitalization. Flinn 1986a applies Bridwell's revision typology to papers written by Mary and other sixth graders.

4 Bob

Case Study of a Basic Writer

Working with computers in a writing community brought Bob almost immediate improvement in his writing skills. For one of his first assignments, Bob was asked to write a letter to a friend about an unfair rule. Bob wrote about not being allowed to wear parachute pants to school on dress-up day. His letter is almost illegible due to a combination of spelling and handwriting problems. That same week, Bob wrote a description of a shell in his journal. This time, Peggy Ryan assigned a peer partner to help him mark the correct spellings on his draft. She also gave him time to type a revision at the computer. The difference between Bob's first two writing samples—one on his own, one with the WritingLand's social and electronic support—is dramatic (fig. 4).

It might seem that Bob could have done just as well proofreading by hand, with a peer partner to help with spelling. Actually, this might be true for Mary, but not for Bob. He found it very hard to recopy accurately; he often created new errors when he corrected the old ones. The computer kept his good text intact, so for the first time ever he could make real headway in proofreading. The printout allowed him to see more clearly what needed fixing. And he felt proud of the finished product because the computer circumvented his poor handwriting.

Although I have been saying that the computer is just a tool—not a magical "good writing" machine—Bob is one writer who almost disproves the point. Almost. Because even a neat, correctly spelled printout shows Bob's weaknesses in development, organization, sentence structure, and style. But if I were in Bob's predicament, I would much sooner face those more challenging issues if I had a computer to aid me in controlling the cosmetics.

At the time we worked together Bob was twelve, a year older than many of his classmates. Peggy Ryan had also taught his second-grade class. At that time Bob was having both academic and personal problems (he repeated the grade). This year, she found his attitude to

Geswhat, My mom whote let
Me wesr peckhetpans, when its
desup day at school! She think
you shoudet go out of the houes with them on!
I thing I shoud be able to were
whatere I wont, Espoley when
it desapdays. I thing I shoud tell her!

THE AUGER SHELL IS LIGHT BEIGE
COLOR WITH 16 BUMPS. WHEN YOU LOOK
AT THE OPENING OF THE SHELL IT LOOK
LIKE A GIANT SLIDE.ON THE OUT SIDE
IT LOOKS LIKE A DRILL OR A TORNADO.

Fig. 4. Bob's first handwritten and computer drafts.

be much more positive, though his skills remained weak. In all his
academic subjects, Bob was at the bottom of the sixth-grade class.[1] I
wondered how he would respond to the freedom, and the immersion
in literacy, of this WritingLand community.

Now let's watch Bob early in the year while he is writing a story
from the point of view of a stingray. He sits in a characteristic posture,
curled sideways at his chair-desk, left arm hanging loose, right hand
scrawling in a journal on his lap. This first draft shows his usual poor
spelling: *fleras* for "furious," *expesly* for "especially." His teacher hands
him a spelling dictionary, which lists each word along with several
more-or-less plausible misspellings. (A spelling checker, had it been
available, could have provided the same kind of support more effi-
ciently.) After correcting his draft, Bob enters a final copy at the
keyboard. His peer partner sits with him, dictating spelling words
from the draft. With this help, Bob completes a two-paragraph story
to print out and share:

> HI, I AM SAMMY THE STINGRAY. I LIKE TO CAMOUFLAGE
> MY SELF AND GO TO THE BEACH AND STING PEAPLE. ITS
> FUN, ESPECIALLY WHEN ITS A STUPED SOME KID.
> ONE DAY WHEN I WAS AT THE BEACH EATING SUPP/ER
> SOME KID SPEPPED ON ME. WHAT NERVE! NO STINGRAY
> SHOULD GET TREATED LIKE THAT, ESPECIALLY ME! RIGHT
> WHEN I WENT TO STING THAT TWERP HE STEPPED ON ME
> AGAIN I WAS FURIOUS SO WHEN I SONG HIM I USED ALL
> MY STRENGH. HIS MOM AND DAD RUSHED HIM TO THE
> HOSPITAL. SO I NEVER STUNG ANYBODY AGAIN. ADULTS
> DONT COUNT.

What is striking in this paper is the strong, natural voice: *Right when
I went to sting that twerp he stepped on me again. I was furious.* Although
Bob has used the computer only to recopy his handwritten text with
spelling corrections, the revision reads like a transformation. His original
eighteen misspellings in 100 words created more than a surface
annoyance; as Mina Shaughnessy (1977) saw among adult basic writers,
errors become a "minefield" through which readers as well as writers
fear to pass. With the computer—sometimes after miscopying a couple
of times—Bob can correct most of his errors and let Sammy's voice
be heard.

Right from the start, Bob has been attracted to the computers. But
he doesn't feel the same enthusiasm for writing. He seems to tolerate
writing, and my questions, for the sake of using the computer. During
my visits he is cooperative but reticent, seldom volunteering to chat
or to share his work in progress.

Reading and writing have never played a big role in Bob's life. At the start of the year, he had trouble describing his taste in books, mentioning S. E. Hinton's *The Outsiders* because "it seemed like it could happen but it didn't." Bob reported that he seldom read books at home ("I should read more, I guess"), but he does read the newspaper, especially the sports and crime reports. He reads mainly when there is nothing on television, adding, "I watch cable TV a lot." About midyear Bob's attitude started to change. He discovered computer magazines, which became his regular free-choice reading in class. He finds them so appealing that on occasion he even buys one of his own.

Bob's self-sponsored writing has been as limited as his reading. It consists mainly of letters to his father and uncle who live out of state. When asked if he ever writes stories or poems outside of school, he chuckles, "No." Yet Bob can describe his own writing process quite explicitly. He usually writes a first draft in his journal "because it's faster" and then types his final copy on the computer "because it's neater." He feels the best thing about word processing is that "you can't lose the paper. It's stored on the disk and you get it back neatly on paper." (Clearly, Bob has not yet experienced the trauma of losing text file electronically.)

Between drafts, Bob pens in revisions, often using peer response from a partner: "I read out loud and he listens. Then he'll look at it to see if there are any spelling errors and he'll listen to see if it sounds right." Most of the year, Bob's writing process follows this pattern: *pencil draft → peer proofreading → computer recopying*—usually with additional cycles of proofreading before the final printed copy.

Bob's major concern in revision is spelling. As aids, Bob uses the small dictionary in his folder, the spelling dictionary, the big classroom dictionary, his peers, and his teacher. Some words he can fix by himself: "by experience—because they don't look right." Still, he finds the editing process frustrating—it's made bearable only by the computer.

The picture that emerges is one that any teacher of basic writers will recognize. Bob does not see himself as a reader or a writer. He uses these skills when he must, but his performance depends a great deal on whether he finds a purpose of his own for reading or writing. Much more than Mary, Bob needs the support of a WritingLand environment. Without the computer, without a peer editor, without a spelling dictionary, without a teacher who cares about his individual interests, without the computer magazines, Bob's life would be almost devoid of reading or writing.

Bob's Writing Process

When his class was given a news clipping about a boy who caught a burglar, Bob decided to be the burglar. It is interesting to watch how Bob, a basic writer, worked through his paper. On this occasion, he was asked to start writing his story directly at the computer—not his preferred process. He brought no handwritten notes to the workstation. I watched as he typed, very slowly but quite steadily, correcting a few errors as he went along: *I nockt* became *I nocked,* and *w hen* was joined together.

After twenty minutes Bob announced that he was done and saved his file. Peggy Ryan, with a glance at his printout, replied, "Okay, you have your ideas down, but you have ten more minutes to get ready for a session with your writing partner." She called his attention to the "five W's" and to a list of suggested peer-response questions. As we might expect, Bob had trouble applying his teacher's suggestions independently. He asked what the five W's were (the topic of the day's lesson), then after a brief reminder said, "Oh, yeah, I know," and set to work. After adding a final sentence, he printed out this seventy-six-word draft:

> I WAS WALKING IN THE NEABERHOOD AND I saw that thir car lights wher on so I nocked but no one asered so I broke the wendo and went in.The kid must of thoght I was robing the house but I was not. When I was in his room looking for some one the cop's come and taken me away.I now I am inasent and i tryed to tell them but thay whoud not lissen.

Next, Bob met with his writing partner for half an hour, marking changes with pen directly on the printout (fig. 5, upper portion). These revisions dealt mainly with surface features, including ten spelling corrections and two verb form changes. He made no changes in units larger than the single word.[2]

Bob started his final session at the computer by misspelling his file name, so he had to struggle to retrieve his file. Watching him, I noticed that he handled cursor movements well but still hunted for letters on the keyboard and went through long pauses while rereading the screen or printout. Though his production was very slow, he succeeded in typing most of his planned corrections. He completed what for him was a rather extended writing process: *teacher input → discussion → computer draft → teacher conference → pencil revision → peer proofreading → computer recopying → conference.*

The result was a seventy-eight word paragraph (fig. 5, lower portion) with four spelling, two wrong word, one apostrophe, and two verb

I WAS WALKING IN THE NE~~A~~BERHOOD *gh* Neighborhood

AND I saw that th~~i~~r *eir* car lights wher *were* on so

I nocked but no one a~~s~~ered *nsw* so I broke

the wendo *indow* and went in.The kid must of

tho~~u~~ght *u* I was rob~~i~~ng *b* the house but I

was not. When I was in his room

looking for some one the cop's c~~o~~me *a*

had and taken me away.I~~k~~now I am in~~p~~sent *e*

a i tryed to tell them but th~~e~~y *e*

wouldn't whoud ~~not~~ lis~~s~~en. *t*

I was walking in the neighborhood

and I saw that their car lights were

on,so I nocked but no one answered so

I broke the window and went in.The kid

must of thought I was robbing the

house but I was not. When I was in his

room looking for some one then the

cop's come and taken me away. I now Iam

iniesent a i tryed to tell them but

they whoud not listen.

Fig. 5. Bob's revisions marked during peer conference.

form errors remaining (four of these errors had been corrected in pen but not entered on the computer). Although he accidentally joined two words (*Iam*), no other new errors were created at the keyboard. This is a real gain over Bob's usual dilemma when recopying by hand.

Bob's revision process does not show a thoughtful reseeing of his story. Unlike Mary, he has difficulty applying feedback and working through drafts to develop a paper. He knows how to use proofreading suggestions, but even with ample time and peer support, he seldom ventures into substantive changes. Bob does not tune in to his writing partner the way he tunes in to the computer.

After Bob finished writing his news story, we watched a replay of his session with COMPTRACE (then on its very first trial). I was struck by the way he observed the software and pointed out when it got stuck or off track. My own attention was set on trying to adjust the program, so our discussion that day was somewhat disjointed. This actually proved to be an advantage. Instead of relating to Bob as a teacher, expert, or authority figure, I wound up in the classic anthropologist's role of the well-meaning but not-too-bright outsider who fumbles around until the natives feel sorry and offer to help! This incident was the first breakthrough in our relationship.

The Romance of Technology

For Christmas Bob received what he wanted most: a microcomputer. Although his Commodore 64 did not have a printer or word-processing software and was used primarily for games, the computer changed Bob's approach to both writing and reading. One day in January, I wrote in my fieldnotes that he seemed much more verbal and animated than usual as he told me about his new machine. He explained that the keyboard had looser action than the Apple at school and that he spent hours working on it "until Mom kick[ed] me off."

During the next few months, each of Bob's major pieces of writing would involve computers in some way. When given a class assignment to create and sell an invention, he drew a desk with computer and printer that collapsed into a portable briefcase. The idea reminded me of the little toys that transform into cars, robots, cassettes, and rockets. But Bob's invention was based on a real laptop portable that he had read about.

"It's sharp. It's a computer that's only THIS big" [gesturing about 6 inches by 8 inches]. It has a little tape built in and a printer. The printer is just about like those calculator rolls, you know, but it works. I read about it in that magazine *Onami* or something."

"Omni?" I suggested.

"Yeah," he replied.

By February I noted that Bob had become an avid reader of computer magazines. His teacher kept a big rack stocked with material for free reading and for use in generating creative writing ideas. She had always collected nature, travel, and science periodicals, all of them full of color photos, but this year she added computer magazines. Bob sometimes spent a whole period reading them. One day he brought *Commodore Power Play* to school, explaining proudly, "It's just for *my* computer." We chatted about printers, software, and synthesizers.

In March the sixth graders were asked to invent a super hero, starting with a drawing and a profile listing occupation, sex, age, race, and special powers. Bob drew a muscular man identified as *computer progamer, male, age 30, Orintal*. He explained that his hero was a "genius" with computers.

Eventually, Bob became something of a computer expert in his WritingLand. As one of the few students to own a computer, he knew enough to help others with the equipment. When the class tried out some grammar software, Bob did not say much about subordinate clauses but he was quick to coach: "Turn it off in back. No, not the screen, the computer. Now press 'control . . . reset.' " This was a distinctly new role for Bob. I had spent two days following his class through all their subjects from math to religion, and he was the lowest performer in every subject but art. He was always quiet, speaking out only to ask for more time to complete his work. The computer seemed to give him a new sense of confidence.

My COMPTRACE program, which developed through a series of malfunctions and modifications, gave him still more reason to feel like an expert. All the students learned to be patient with composing sessions that failed to play back or that crashed midway through their best revision. But of the eight middle school writers working on the case studies, only Bob showed an active interest in the program and in figuring out what went wrong.

One day, after successfully replaying one of his sessions, I accidentally let COMPTRACE save the revised text, overwriting the first draft. When I explained the mishap, Bob's eyes widened sympathetically. Then he gave me some advice:

> Bob: "Well, what you could do is just put one of those little silver tapes over the notch and then it wouldn't do that."
>
> Zeni: "Will the program still read my files?"
>
> Bob: "Yeah, you can read it and even copy it. You just can't erase

any of the information. I know because my Dad got real mad
at me when I lost a program I was copying without a write-
protect tape."

Of course he was right, and his solution was far simpler than my
asking the programmer to modify the software, as I had planned to
do. On my next visit I showed Bob a sheet of write-protect tabs, and
I said I'd think of him whenever I used one.

Gradually, Bob's romance with technology seemed to transfer to a
new sense of pride and ownership in his writing. Near the end of the
year, he filled out an attitude scale. One item asked him to rate his
own writing in comparison with that of his peers: *below average,
average,* or *above average.* Without hesitation, Bob checked *average*—a
label I don't think he would have considered in September.

Scaffolding—Peers, Teacher, Tools

Bob and Mary work in the same WritingLand environment, but they
use the community's resources quite differently. The contrast is most
apparent in their peer conferences.

Bob marked little on his drafts other than spelling corrections, even
when a partner suggested more global improvements. Yet the help of
a spelling coach was something he used and valued. Dave and Ben,
both good writers, were his usual peer partners. Peggy Ryan chose
Bob's writing partners carefully: "He needs someone who can find his
misspellings but point them out gently, without laughing at him."

For Bob, editing without peer support was a frustrating ordeal.
Once, for a class assignment, he was asked to revise a brief, error-
filled story in a single half-hour session at the computer. He scrolled
through the story repeatedly, searching the screen but making few
corrections. As we watched, I asked him to explain his revision process
with COMPTRACE:

> *Zeni:* "Bob, when you're reading through like this, what's going
> on in your head? What are you looking for?"
>
> *Bob:* "I'm just trying to search and sometimes . . . you read through
> it; when you can't find anything you get furious. I feel like I'm
> just gonna punch, just punch a hole in the wall!"
>
> *Zeni:* "Are you furious because you know there's something there
> and you can't see it?"
>
> *Bob:* "Yeah, you can't see it. And sometimes you'll read that word
> about sixteen times and you still—and then you finally find
> out that it's spelled wrong."

Although he relied on spelling partners, Bob seldom collaborated with a peer in composing an entire paper, something that Mary and Linda so often did. On the rare occasions when he tried collaborating, he tended to be passive, waiting for his partner to supply the ideas. Once he found himself in a different role as he tried to design a futuristic car with a peer who had broken his wrist. The circumstances required Bob to be the scribe. During prewriting, he carefully drew the car and talked with his partner about the marvelous things it could do. When I walked over, both boys shared their ideas readily. But Bob wrote very little down until he was prodded by his teacher. Nevertheless the boys did eventually finish a collaborative paragraph. Their process was *collaborative drawing → oral planning → pencil draft*. I wondered if Bob was so obviously the weaker member of any pair that it made true collaboration feel awkward.

In December, a Christmas tree tale gave me a chance to see how Bob applied feedback from an adult. The draft was handwritten over a two-day period. Spelling corrections were marked and a final copy was typed on the computer. Here is the first draft:

> Hi, I am a Christmas tree living in the back lard of the four nicest peaple in the world.
> One day when I lived in the forest, 3 men started two cut some of my frinds down. Why I woundered. One guy stared to cut me down. He wore a very hevy fenle shirt, sapenders, and blou geans with holes in the nee's and he had a long red berd going down to his stamike. he must be from Indeana I thout. he tied me up with my some of in the brack of a pickup truck. When we got to were ever we wher going. I looked around and thir where 100's of trees all cut down in a very crowed spot.
> The 3th Day I was thir a famaly of came looking for a chrismas tree. They took me home and stuck ornaments on me.
> 12:00 A.M. Chistmas Morning is when they stared to put pezants under me. At ten Am. the children stared to open ther pesant's. then went to ther gramal and 3 hours later they came back and stared to take me out side and they planted me back in the ground.

Peggy Ryan and I laughed with Bob over the caricature of the Hoosier from Indiana. Then, in a brief conference, I asked some questions that prompted him to develop the story more. "I like the idea that the tree survives; that's an interesting twist. But I wonder how that could happen if it's cut down? That part confuses me." I also asked for more information on why the children changed their minds and put the tree outside right after decorating it.

The next day, Bob met with Dave to correct his spelling. Bob carefully wrote out a list of all his misspelled words and their correct forms. Then he went to the computer to revise. His final story shows most of the intended surface changes, plus two revisions that affect meaning. The statement *One guy started to cut me down*, in his draft, became *One guy started to dig me up*, in his revision. Also, the confusing reference to visiting grandma is omitted at the end, and the children wait until *one week later* before planting the tree back in the ground. Both these changes respond to the questions I asked in conference; the revisions make the plot somewhat more coherent. The paper reflects Bob's usual process, with increased response bringing a bit more development: *pencil draft → peer proofreading → conference → computer draft → peer proofreading*.

When Bob did not have this much direct support from peers or adults, he often found that his composing process became blocked. Slides and videotapes show his lanky frame draped across his chair, a shock of sandy hair almost covering his eyes. Sometimes he sat in this position without writing. One day I watched him stare at the journal where he was planning a story and produce just a few lines in a class period. Although he had met earlier with Dave for feedback, he had not written down any suggestions, claiming the ideas were all in his head.

During the next few weeks he gained momentum, adding episodes and characters to that narrative. "Spy Hunter," based on a video game, became his most ambitious and successful work that year (fig. 6). When it was done, I asked him about the day he felt blocked. He described what happened:

> *Bob:* "You know, you're kind of thinking about the weekend and looking at the clock and you're thinking of anything but your paper."
>
> *Zeni:* "How did you break that block? All writers feel that way at times, they even call it 'writer's block.'"
>
> *Bob:* "Well, I got a little more done in my journal and then I went to the computer and put it in. I was just sitting there thinking about the weekend and I go to my grandma's and watch TV and Sunday there's wrestling. And I got the idea of putting a wrestler in my story."
>
> *Zeni:* "Neat! So when your mind wandered it actually brought you back to your story. Now you wrote this part directly on the computer, right? How did it feel?"
>
> *Bob:* "Okay. You know I think on the computer you can't really waste time because other people are waiting and Mrs. Ryan will kick you off. Also, she said to me, 'Bob, you better get this done because [Zeni] will be here tomorrow'—so I just did all of this." [holds up long printout]

Zeni: "So you work well under pressure?"

Bob: "Yeah, maybe. When you write at a desk you can kind of daydream and waste more time."

I wasn't sure whether to feel glad or guilty about my own influence on Bob's composing rhythm. But I noted that his writer's block was broken first from the inside (daydreaming about the TV wrestler) and second from the outside (the pressure of computer time and research meetings).

Bob's story for his class mythology project found his thoughts blocked again. On the first day he seemed abstracted, even at the computer, and produced just a sixty-word text in thirty minutes:

A long time a go Hades was apointed smartest slave to find a way to get useles people out of the under world. but the slave could think of anything becouse of Zues. The slave said,if you can get the chest of power you can make zues do what ever you want he to do. What dose the chest do.

My fieldnotes describe Bob's process as he completed the first sentence: "Types *Hades*, long pause, looks in book, stares into space, adjusts chair, tilts screen, deletes *Hades*, mutters 'I can't think.' " After five more minutes, and three more words, I decided to say something:

Zeni: "You're stuck, Bob, aren't you."

Bob: "Yes.

Zeni: "What can you do when you get stuck like that?"

Bob: "I dunno, just sit and look at it and wait until the ideas come."

Zeni: "Well, okay, but that could take a while. Have you ever tried to just write any old thing—just words, even if they're silly—to get moving? With the computer you can pick the good stuff to use later."

Bob: "Yeah, but you can't just write fast on this."

Apparently Bob was desperate, so he did try freewriting at the computer, producing the next three lines before his time ran out. (The image of the slave who couldn't "think of anything" fits exactly the mood of this writing!) Once more, his writer's block was broken by an outside suggestion.

While watching Bob's progress during the year, I kept thinking of what Vygotsky (1978) calls the "zone of proximal development." Vygotsky's "zone" is the gap between what a learner can do independently, and what is possible with the help of an adult or more-experienced child. The Russian psychologist says that we should focus

SPY HUNTER

ONE DAY A BOY NAMED BILL WAS PLAYING SPY HUNTER ON HIS
COMPUTER. HE HAD A SPECIAL COPY THAT NO ONE HAD. IT WAS
GIVEN TO HIM BY HIS LATE DAD THAT JUST PAST AWAY 3 WEEKS
AGO.HIS DAD COULD DO ANYTHING WITH A COMPUTER. HIS DAD
TOLD HIM THAT IF HE GOT TO A CERTAIN PLACE THAT HE WOUD
GET A SURPRISE.THAT NIGHT, NOT THINKING OF WHAT HIS DAD
TOLD HIM, HE WAS REACHING SCORES THAT HE NEVER REACHED
BEFORE.THEN A LIGHT CAME OUT OF THE DISK DRIVE. HE FOLOWED
IT THROUGH THE HALLWAY OUT THE DOOR TO THE DRIVEWAY.
ON THE DRIVEWAY
WAS THE SAME CAR THAT WAS ON SPY HUNTER. HE OPENS THE
DOOR, AND GITS IN. THEN THE HOLE DASHBORD LIT-UP.THERE WAS
A LITTLE SLOTT, ALL THE SOUDEN A DISK CAME OUT, ON IT WAS
LOAD*,8 HIT RETURN, IN THE CORNER OF THE DISK IT SAID LOAD
ON YOUR COMPUTER.

HE WENT INSIDE AND RAN IT. IT WAS LIKE A BOOK OF
INSTRUCTIONS. IT SAID EVERYTHING YOU NEED TO NOW TO RUN
THE CAR.

_____   EPISODE 1#

THE

MYSTERY

OF THE

DISAPPEARING

BANK TRUCK

ONE DAY, AFTER HE READ THE DISK, HE WAS TRYING-OUT HIS
CAR ON THE COUNTRY ROAD IN THE MIDDLE OF A FOREST THAT
WENT ON FOR MILES.

Fig. 6. "Good writing" = length + spelling.

THEN THE ALARM WENT OFF. HE REMEMBERED THAT MEANT TO
CALL THE WEAPONS WAR VAN. HE CALLED RIGHT AWAY. THE
DRIVER MACK SAID, THAR ARE TWO MISSING BANK TRUCK THAT
DISAPERED TODAY. FIND THEM AND THE CRUKES IN THREE DAYS.

THE TIME WAS 5:00 ON A FRIDAY. HE DID NOT HAVE MUCH TIME.
IT IS GOING TO BE HARD HE THOUGHT.

SO HE STARTED.

HE WENT HOME AND CHECKED OUT FOR ANY ESCAPED
CRIMINALS AND THERE WAS—FAST ED AND BIG JOE. FAST ED WAS
FAMOUS FOR ROBBING BANK TRUCK AND BIG JOE IS HIS BODY
GUARD. HE USED TO BE A WRESTLER UNTIL HIS WORST ENAMY BEET
HIM. HIS NAME WAS ROUGH RALPH.

IT MUST BE FAST ED HE THOUGHT. BUT WHERE IS HE AND IF I
FIND HIM HOW WILL CATCH HIM.

I GOT IT! I WILL GET RALPH TO HELP ME. SO HE WENT DOWN TO
THE GYM.

THERE HE WAS LIFTING WEIGHTS. I WENT UP AND ASKED HIM
AND HE SAID YES.
SO I WENT HOME AND WENT TO BED AT 8:00.

THE NEXT DAY I GOT UP AND RIGHT I REMEMBERED THAT FAST
ED,S MOM LIVES IN THE LONG FORIST. SO HE GOT RALPH AT THE
GYM AND WENT TO THE FORIST.

AFTER A LITTEL BIT WE WERE THER. WE GOT OUT AND BROKE IN.

RALPH TOUCK CARE OF IT AND THE POLICE CAME.

Fig. 6. *Continued.*

our teaching on this zone, guiding the child through the next level of development.

Working on his own, Bob continued at a very low skill level. But with support, he could perform at a higher level while still keeping ownership of his writing. Such support came to him through the computer (neatness and ease of correction), through peer response (finding misspellings, audience reactions), and through conferences with teacher or researcher (plot alternatives, reflection on his own process). Sometimes I thought he was growing more in confidence than in writing skills, but with help he completed some pieces that made him proud.

When he retook the California Achievement Test in the fall of seventh grade, Bob showed that his gains were, in fact, substantial. During a year in this WritingLand, Bob had made an average of two years' progress in all the reading and language subskills; his scores rose from roughly a third-grade to a fifth-grade level. In math and science, his scores actually rose to grade level, perhaps due in part to his romance with technology and the computer magazines. The computer and the classroom social context helped Bob read and write with some success in his zone of proximal development. This WritingLand was preparing him to enter the literate world.

Good Writing = Length + Spelling

While the computer seemed to make a real difference in the quality of Bob's writing, I don't think it changed his personal model of what makes a piece of writing good. If Mary's model of "good writing" was description, Bob seemed to work toward an equally-consistent ideal of his own. We can see it operating in many of his writing decisions.

Most of the changes he made in his papers dealt with mechanics, especially spelling. On one class assignment, Bob made a total of twelve changes, six of them at the surface level. This represents a typical, low-skilled revision pattern. Calkins (1980) calls it *refining* rather than revising for meaning. Research conducted with basic writers shows that by focusing on surface correctness, those writers often fail to improve their texts either in mechanics or in overall quality.[3] Such writers seem to believe that the key to good writing is good spelling.

There are, however, two elements in Bob's formula for good writing. Along with spelling, Bob is very conscious of length. He explains that the sentences need work in a story he is revising because "I think I corrected some of them, but they stopped, I mean the sentences were too short. They should have made a run-on sentence for a couple of them." He adds, "Some of these other sentences . . . should have periods . . . to break them up, cause you don't want big sentences but you also don't want about twenty sentences." This comment suggests that his concept of the correct sentence is based on length rather than on syntax, leading to what Flower and others (1986) call a "maxim" for revision (50). According to Bob's maxim, a correct sentence is not too short (fragment) and not too long (run-on). With his rough maxim, he fixes a sentence fragment, but he doesn't manage to insert any periods to break up a run-on. Bob judges the overall merit of a story according to its length. When asked what else might be improved, he volunteers,

> This wasn't too long of a story. I think that at the end he . . . should have wrote a little bit more instead of ending it so quickly.

Bob can identify with the problem:

> I think that it would have been a lot better story if this person would have made it longer at the end. . . . I know I do that a lot too, you know, I'll get tired of writing a story so I'll just kind of end it real quick.

"Spy Hunter," Bob's most ambitious piece, was a great success according to his model of good writing. It developed over a period of six weeks. Bob kept adding episodes until the finished tale contained 450 words in four pages of draft-mode printout (fig. 6).

Bob was proud of "Spy Hunter." One day, when trying to punctuate dialogue in separate paragraphs, he wound up with big spaces between every piece. I fixed the spacing for him, but he thanked me with a hint of regret. He had enjoyed the outpouring of continuous paper— and the comments of his classmates: "Whose paper is *that*? Bob's?" The computer had accidentally let him achieve one of his goals—a really long paper.

Parts of his story were first composed by hand, but most of it was composed directly on the keyboard. Written in the spring, "Spy Hunter" represents a new level of fluency. Bob now seemed to make the computer his chosen writing tool as well as his chosen editor.

As usual, during editing sessions Bob worked with a partner to fix his unorthodox spelling. His final text (fig. 6) is a major achievement in his ability to control mechanics. Consider the opening paragraph as it was first drafted at the computer:

> ONE DAY A BOY NAMED BILL WAS PLAYING SPY HUNTER
> ON HIS COMPUTER. HE HAD A SPECIAL COPY THAT NO

ONE HAD. IT WAS GAVE TO HIM BY HIS LATE DAD THAT
JUST PAST AWAY 3 WEEKI AGO. HIS DAD COUD DO ANY-
THING WITH A COMPUTER. HIS DAD TOLD HIM THAT IF
HE GOT TO A SERTON PLACE THAT HE WOUD GET A
SURPREZE. THAT NIGHT, NOT THINKING OF WHAT HIS DAD
TOLD HIM, WAS REACHING SCORES THAT HE NEVER
REACHED BEFORE. THEN A LIGHT CAME OUT OF THE DISK.
HE FOLOWED IT THEW THE HALLWAY OUT THE DOOR TO
THE DRIVEWAY. ON THE DRIVEWAY WAS THE SAME CAR
THAT WAS ON SPY HUNTER.

Throughout the year, Bob continued to revise his papers according
to the same implicit formula: *good writing = length + spelling*. The
computer helped him do the two things he valued most. Since he
judged his content mainly in terms of length, he used the computer
to add material, episode by episode, to the end of a text. And with
each printout he could catch a few more spelling errors and remain
confident that he would not undo his previous corrections through
recopying.

At this stage in his development, Bob is not ready to use all the
options available in his classroom. He needs—and gets—support to
work at his own level and toward his own goals. At the same time,
Bob is part of a WritingLand community and is thereby exposed to
more mature notions of writing and reading. If he continues in this
type of environment, he can count on that social support to guide him
forward.

Notes

1. Bob's fall writing sample (the parachute pants letter) was given the
bottom rating: 2 on a 2–12 scale. His California Achievement Tests showed
skills at about the third-grade level, with national percentiles between 9 and
14 on all reading and language subtests.

2. For a detailed analysis of Bob's revision pattern, using Lillian Bridwell's
typology, see Flinn 1986a.

3. For research on older writers and their approach to error, see Shaughnessy (1977), Perl (1979), Sommers (1980), and Bridwell (1980).

5 The Writing Process

Watching Bob and Mary and other students at work suggests how individual, even fickle, the "composing process" can be. My observations helped me understand why researchers have not found a one-to-one correspondence between the use of computers, the process of working through papers, and the quality of the writing produced. Yet, in this chapter I want to step back from the case study close-ups to reflect on what we do know about the writing process—from published research as well as from our own classrooms—and how the computer may affect that process.

"Process" is an elusive concept. The early process theorists, such as Murray (1968), Emig (1971), and Britton (1975), spoke of several fairly distinct "stages" in the writing of a paper. Many teachers have adopted these linear models under such names as "prewriting," "writing," and "rewriting." In its purest form, a linear model suggests that a writer generates ideas, quickly sets them down from start to finish in a first draft, then goes back to revise until the piece is right (fig. 7).

If we consider how we, or our students, write, this model appears much too simple. By 1978, Don Murray was suggesting a distinction between "internal revision" (playing with changes while still writing a first draft) and "external revision" (going back to revise a completed draft). Most current theorists say that the process is not linear but "recursive." They show how the process turns back on itself, muddling the neat linear stages. When I consider and then reject many plans before ever putting pen to paper, do I "revise" my "prewriting"? When I pause amid the final draft to plan a paragraph insert, do I "prewrite" my "rewrite"? The linear categories don't really make sense. Frank Smith (1982) sees the writing process as an ever-changing interaction between the flow of thought and the flow of text (fig. 8).

Through the work of Linda Flower and John Hayes, the idea of "process" has moved still further away from the activity of producing drafts. Flower and Hayes (1981, 372–74) see the writing process as a set of mental operations which a writer can use at any point in the production of a paper. They describe three major cognitive processes: "planning," generating ideas, organizing them, and setting goals;

Fig. 7. Linear stage model of the composing process.

"translating," putting ideas into words either on paper or in speech; and "reviewing," reading, judging, and changing what has been written. Although more planning occurs in the early phases of writing a paper and more reviewing in the later ones, all processes are available at all times. With Flower and Hayes's model, saying that I "review" my "plans" or that I "plan" my final-draft changes *does* make sense (fig. 9).

Cognitive models do better than linear stages in representing the complexity of the writing process. Yet they oversimplify in a different way by making the process mental rather than social. In 1981, when Flower and Hayes used the term "environment" (369), they limited their scope to an assignment or problem and a developing draft. What about the social environment of the classroom or workplace? Their data were drawn from a laboratory environment where adult writers were given a specific task, a short time limit, no instructional support, and no chance for peer response or leisurely rethinking. I'm reluctant to apply to students a model derived from a setting that violates what we know about learning to write. In her recent work, Linda Flower (1989) delves into "context" and "culture" and "social process"—but only as they can be inferred from what individual writers say to a researcher.

I would like to reconsider the "writing process" as it has appeared during action research among students and teachers in WritingLand environments. I will begin by looking at drafts and printouts and their fuzzy relationship to writing processes. Then I will look closer at "planning," "translating," and "reviewing"—starting with the cognitive model, but fleshed out with the affective and social processes of writers in computer-equipped settings. Fig. 10 is my attempt to show this fuller, contextual model of the writing process.

The Draft?

The production of "drafts," even multiple drafts, has never been a sure sign of the composing process. We have all seen students who merely recopy successive drafts with neater handwriting and straighter margins. Today it is clear that the very concept of "draft" fails to fit the composing processes of students who write with computers.

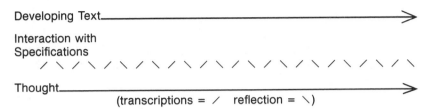

Fig. 8. Interactive model of the composing process. (Adapted from: *Writing and the Writer* by Frank Smith, p. 116. Copyright 1982 by Lawrence Erlbaum Associates, Inc. Used with permission.)

During our action research, students planned and revised and printed out again and again. But watching them, I realized that printed copies cannot be equated with drafts. One writer may work on a paper for two or three sessions, making many changes, yet never printing it out until the end. Another may insist on a printout after every session. One writer trudges through a text sequentially, revising from first page to last, then prints it out. Another makes the cursor fly about the text, replacing and moving passages, printing out often to keep track of organization. One composes for a while, prints, then clears the screen and starts from scratch. Another makes several printouts that differ by just a word or a comma. If we turn from students to adult writers, the notion of "draft" seems more alien still; in a high-tech office, writing may be generated, revised, and transmitted in a "paperless environment."

Our teachers have found that requiring two or three "drafts" as evidence of the writer's process no longer means very much. Even when a student prints every few minutes, we cannot trace the writing process through the hard copies. Any changes made at the keyboard and then discarded or changed again will vanish before the text is printed out, so we cannot see the work of "internal revision." (My solution in the case studies was COMPTRACE, but a keystroke catcher is hardly practical for everyday assignments.)

Fieldnotes from our research show that students working with computers used the term "draft" less and less as they grew accustomed to the new tools. They spoke of "class," "day," or "printout" to identify points in the production of their papers. In March, an eighth grader handed me a thick folder containing a collaborative history report she and a friend had written at the computer.

> *Zeni:* "It looks like you and Emily did a lot of revising."
> *Student:* "Yes, we had several . . . er. . . ."
> *Zeni:* "Drafts?"
> *Student:* "Well, sort of. They're just like stages in the process."

When the computer is used as a writing tool, the last remnants of a rigid, linear model of composing break down. As writers, teachers, and researchers, we can no longer cut apart the "stages." The process seems fluid, with a sequence of drafts or printouts being shaped by a writer's individual work habits.

Sounds wonderful. . . . But of course there is a catch. The computer makes it easy to revise, easy to develop a paper through a full, recursive process. It also makes it easy to confuse a neat new printout with a real revision. People who use word processing must beware the computer-generated illusion of process: Paul reads over a printout full of comments by insightful peers and a sensitive teacher. He boots the word processor, calls up his file, and fixes the easy stuff—spelling errors, paragraph breaks, word choice (provided the reader has suggested a better word). Perhaps he even adds a few details in response to marginal questions. A couple of keypunches and Paul's "revision" is saved and printed out.

Brad Heger encountered these nondrafts in an advanced ninth-grade course requiring multiple revisions. When his students began using computers, his paper load suddenly increased. New "drafts" were coming in just a day after he had returned a set of papers (or sooner if a student could get to the lab at lunchtime). At first the teacher was impressed by this new diligence, but when he read the drafts he changed his mind. Students had taken advantage of the neat reprinting that can be done by a computer so that they could avoid the broad rethinking that can be done only by a writer. Here is Brad Heger's reflection:

> We have all known students who have used their poor handwriting to camouflage their poor spelling skills. Now we face the danger of students who use their word processors to camouflage their poor revision skills. Thus it seems that a cautionary note is in order: while the computer makes the manipulation of text easier for an accomplished writer (or for a fast learner), in the hands of the unsophisticated writer (or the slower learner) it also makes superficiality of revision a greater danger. . . . Students who do not revise well do not know *how* to revise well. They do not need to learn only the split and glue commands for their software, but *when* the split and glue commands should be used. . . . Teachers must take care to go beyond teaching pencil sharpening. Teaching word processing cannot be substituted for teaching writing process.

He finally warned his students, "I'll be glad to read your revisions and regrade them. But if you waste my time with a patched-up printout, your new grade may be *lower.*" It helped.

A recent article on professional writing (Grow 1988) warns of the

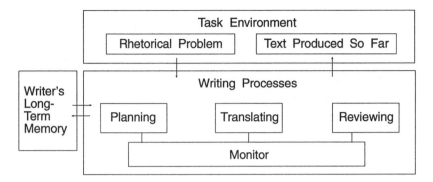

Fig. 9. Cognitive model of the composing process. (Adapted from Flower and Hayes 1981, 370. Used with permission.)

same danger. The computer lets us play with block moves, plug in pieces of old manuscripts, merge collaborators' texts, and fine-tune details to fit a new audience—even professionals may be tempted to throw something together. As an editor, Grow has observed that executives, journalists, and engineers are coming up with prose that no competent writer would have conceived from scratch.

I think we should discuss these dangers with our students and point out examples of sloppy computer-generated "revisions." Gradually, even our less-skilled writers will grow more sophisticated in using the technology, more aware that the power of the process must remain with the writer. Students can learn to use new writing tools responsibly, if we teach them how. To do that, we must understand what really happens in the act of writing and how electronic tools may affect the process.

The Writing Process?

I do not plan to propose some new, improved, computerized version of the writing process. Published research as well as observations of WritingLands suggest that computers do not change the basic components of the process. Whether working by hand or by machine, students collect ideas, plan, draft, use feedback, struggle with writer's block, and feel pride or distress after finishing a paper. But subtly, gradually, the computer penetrates that experience. After a year of working with computers, Cathy Beck observed that her basic writers "seemed to view the Writer's Center as another step in the writing process."

Let's see what happens to that "process" in a WritingLand environment. This chapter will focus on word processing as the essential computer writing tool (chapter 13 will consider some related software that may be useful to writers). My discussion is based on Flower and Hayes's (1981) model of composing, but it is grounded in the data from our own action research in classrooms where students routinely write by word processing.

Planning

The cognitive term "planning" suggests something more deliberate, more directed, than what I actually saw in most elementary and secondary school WritingLands. In an environment that supports the writing process, "planning" can include many styles, from leisurely to pressured. For example, students may talk over ideas for days or weeks before setting them down in text. Peggy Ryan's children often leafed through nature magazines until a picture sparked an idea for a story; then they would claim a computer, set the picture next to the keyboard, and start writing.

My own planning process may be more leisurely still. At a recent institute on teaching writing with computers, one participant led a guided meditation to prepare for writing about an experience with a machine. Closing my eyes, I recalled learning to drive a stick shift car in Germany in 1966. I was young, scared, and mechanically inept. An explanation of clutches and gears confused me more as my engine died at every Heidelberg intersection. At last a friend who shared my love of horseback riding tried a metaphor: my spirited Volkswagen simply wanted to change from a trot (second gear) to a canter (third gear). With a shock of recognition, I was driving. Over the years, I had told that story dozens of times and probably even written about it in a letter or two. But I had never tried to capture what it meant until that summer institute, twenty years later. There I found the theme of my essay: "One good metaphor is worth a thousand words of explanation!"

Perhaps that tale had been "planning" itself in my head all those years. But the term "incubation" (Britton and others 1975, 25–32) seems to fit my process better, as it fits the browsing and talking we see in WritingLands. That's the leisurely style of planning.

Once students get to the keyboard, they tend to feel some pressure to stop incubating and stay on task: "On the computer you can't really waste time because other people are waiting and Mrs. Ryan will kick you off," explained Bob. This pressure may lessen in settings with

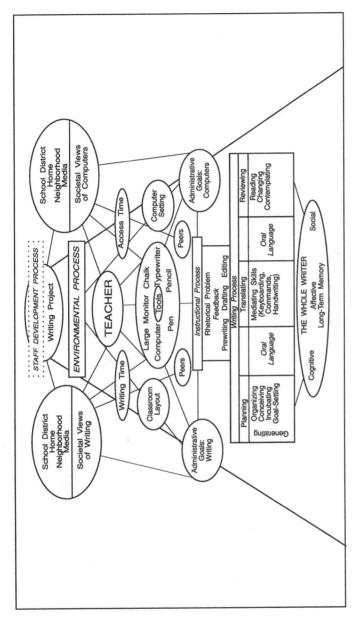

Fig. 10. Contextual model: composing in a WritingLand environment.

many computers, but it is a reality in most schools. So that they learn to balance the need to stay on task with the need to mull over ideas, students can be encouraged to do a good deal of talking and planning by hand before going to the computer.

Under today's conditions, most of the teachers in our project find that prewriting works best with pen and paper. Word processing, limited to a screen of twenty-four lines, does not lend itself to many creative planning techniques. So our students may use drawing, flowcharts, brainstorming, clustering, or webbing to plan out a sense of the whole, and then set their handwritten maps next to the keyboard as they compose.

Although some writers like to start "cold" at the computer with a discovery draft, others find that slow typing interferes with nonstop freewriting. I have watched students hunt for keys or struggle with commands in a way that distracted them from planning and sometimes made them create garbled sentences. Why use computer time for freewriting, which is meant to be sloppy free association? On the other hand, computers work very well for outlines. Anne Wright found that a "preliminary question outline" on the word processor helped organize research papers. Her seniors planned the search by typing some questions about their topics:

> How did apartheid begin?
>
> How do black South Africans live under apartheid?
>
> How do white South Africans live?
>
> What can Americans do?

Then they sought answers to the questions, typing information and quotes in the proper category. As they continued reading, they built their structures, using block functions to revise categories and subcategories. Their teacher reported that their final papers were more coherent than usual, both in organization and in style.

Translating

Cognitive theorists use this term exclusively for the act of putting ideas into words, either orally or on paper. By the middle elementary grades, the average child's handwriting is almost automatic; translating by hand requires little attention. But when inexperienced writers start using the computer, translating is anything but automatic. Keyboarding and software commands claim a great deal of their attention. The writer is reduced to the level of a much younger child who struggles to form the right letters while trying to think what to say. Such mediating skills as handwriting, typing, and knowing software commands need to be considered as part of the composing process in a WritingLand. Should these mediating skills be taught directly or inductively?

Some teachers on our research team set aside a week or two of class time to learn word processing with an on-screen tutorial or to practice keyboarding with a typing program. They hoped this instruction would help students start composing fluently at the keyboard and also lessen the initial stress. In practice, most found it didn't work. Even after such lessons, inexperienced typists who tackle a major paper will tend to get bogged down in hunting and pecking.

It is important to note that the keyboarding crunch seems to be an instructional bottleneck, a phase rather than a fundamental problem. It is a phase in learning (mainly affecting the first encounters with word processing) as well as a phase in development (mainly affecting early adolescents).

Primary school children seldom find typing a problem. Even in the early weeks, they don't complain that it slows them down or stops them from writing long pieces. But consider how primary children write by hand. For many, forming their letters is still a challenge. Words are produced slowly, painstakingly, and mistakes are often fixed by erasing holes into their papers. When transcription by hand is not yet automatic, transcription by machine may actually be faster. (In IBM's "Write to Read" program, first graders eagerly type their very first original pieces of writing.)

Students at a later stage of development, in high school, also rarely complain about keyboarding. Many have already taken touch-typing; others are familiar with the keyboard's visual layout. In our research, we found keyboarding an obstacle mainly in junior high, among writers who transcribe fluently and automatically by hand but who have no prior knowledge of typing. With word processing, their fluency drops and their attention shifts to transcribing rather than communicating. The quickest way through this instructional bottleneck is to compose short, meaningful pieces that call upon the computer's real power: revision.

Reviewing

Since reviewing is not just a final "stage," writers will review plans and first drafts as well as mechanics. Nancy Sommers (1980) aptly defines revision as a process of decision making through which a text evolves.

In a WritingLand, students make such decisions by conferring freely with peers and teachers. Their comments tend to resemble the ones cited by Flower and her research team (1986, 24) in their classification of reviewing activities: our writers "evaluate" their papers, "detect" or "diagnose" problems, and select a "strategy" for making changes. But in the classroom, these cognitive processes depend on social support—remember that both Mary and Bob needed feedback to do a thorough job of revising.

The computer makes all kinds of revision simpler to execute. Studies of revision by Sommers (1980) and Bridwell (1980) identified four operations: addition, deletion, substitution, and reordering. Although these studies dealt with revision by hand, the same four operations apply to revision by computer, which makes all four easier to do. By moving the cursor, writers can add material anywhere in a text without arrows or marginal mazes; the delete key is faster and neater than correction tape, white-out, or eraser; block functions, though somewhat trickier, make it possible to substitute or reorder large chunks of text without retyping.

Once students are even slightly adept with word processing, they find that the computer takes the mechanical drudgery out of revising. One sixth grader, Josh, put it this way:

> I think I'm a lot lazier when I'm writing with a pen and paper because with a pen and paper you have to get your eraser out and scratch out, but with a computer you just move the key and 'bi di di dip'—it's gone!

Word processing supports editing because peers find a double-spaced printout easy to read and easy to mark up. The handwritten comments and revision notes stay visually distinct from the printed draft. The computer is also a special boon to basic writers in proof-reading. Mechanical errors are easier to see, and the ones that continue to lurk in almost-final copy can be fixed without the risk of making new errors in recopying.

In a WritingLand, the computer supports the process by reinforcing the help of peers, teachers, and books. Many of our teachers give a process grade as well as a product grade to students who use these resources. Many validate the often-lengthy process of developing a good paper by displaying its history. Seventh-grade teacher Mary Ann Kelly explains:

> We kept all drafts in "sandwich" form, first handwritten to last printout. The idea that these stacks were quite thick often en-couraged [low-skilled] students that they were really putting out

some work! They could see the revisions, the remarks of their partners (and if they had responded to them or not), and the final copy that satisfied them. Their involvement intensified when they were ready to illustrate with marking pens and bring color to the paper literally. The final product was laminated for a class book.

Then comes the moment when a writer may engage in "contemplation of the product" (Emig 1971, 44). Like Britton's "incubation," Emig's "contemplation" belongs to a more leisurely and more communal world than the timed laboratory experiments of Flower and Hayes. A WritingLand is a place to contemplate as well as to create.

Contemplate, then share: publishing happens whenever writing reaches its audience. "Usually considered to be at the end of a continuum that begins internally and moves to a neatly printed work," publishing is defined by our teachers as "any point on the continuum from self to distant other" (Bollefer, Johnston, and Phillips 1988, 124). Through publication, I may display my work for the world, for my peer group, or for my own pleasure.

The computer gives writers much quicker access to the publishing continuum, from the simplest to the most elegant forms. Multiple printouts can provide cheap, immediate drafts to share with response groups. Computer-assisted graphics and desktop publishing software can help students produce newspapers, comic strips, and story illustrations. Laser-printed books, bound in laminated covers to display at a "Young Authors' Conference," invite the most admiring "contemplation of the product."

Fuel for the Process

Two other issues, often neglected, are central to the composing process. Talking and feeling supply the human energy that is expressed in writing. Adults who are writing an assigned task in a laboratory setting may not need to talk or feel, but students in a writing community do.

Oral Language

Neither cognitive nor linear models of composing list oral language as a major process. But in WritingLand environments, what Britton (1975, 29) calls "good talk" tends to fuel the composing process. Writers may discover their ideas through improvisation, storytelling, or oral rehearsal. Then they may read and reread their texts aloud to an audience, both from the screen and from the printout. Oral language permeates all phases of composing.

Writing at the computer is a social process that is accompanied by a lot of generally on-task talk. For new users, much of that talk deals with keys and commands, rather than with content. A writer leans toward someone at the next workstation and asks, "How do you get it to indent?" The writer's peer may respond by explaining (e.g., "Hit 'TAB' "), by pointing to the key, or by moving closer to demonstrate the command. As writers gain experience, more of the talk deals with the text. Two students may share a single computer and develop entire papers together. Watching children like Mary and Linda collaborate make me recall Suzanne Langer's (1942) theory of the twin roots of human language: babbling play and social interaction. The writing seems to flow naturally from the spontaneous chatter.

Tape recordings of collaborative writing sessions catch all three of the recursive processes: *Planning* can be heard in questions ("What should we write?") as well as in peer coaching ("Put in more details") and in oral rehearsal of specific lines. *Translating* is heard in the click of the keyboard. *Reviewing* is heard in talking about problems, debating alternatives, and reading text aloud from the screen.

Teachers who want to understand the thinking-and-writing process should try listening to a couple of students talking their way through a paper. It can be a fascinating introduction to classroom research on composing.

The Affective Process

I have based this discussion on a cognitive model of composing. Yet the thought of writing—and the thought of computers—must also conjure up feelings in the would-be author. The power of "writer's block," "computerphobia," and "poetic inspiration" warns us not to ignore the affective processes at work in a WritingLand.

For most students, computers seem to generate two responses, both of them positive. First, our writers sense an aura of intelligence and competence. They describe the computer as a metaphor, even a magic formula, for intelligence. Perhaps they are awed to find themselves masters of something called an electronic brain. Even when I have watched them struggle with software, fussing until they solved some technical problem, they have expressed the same sense of intellectual challenge: "I did it!" exulted one eighth-grade girl. A classmate celebrated his triumph by pointing to his head and mouthing, "Brains. . . ."

Our writers engage just as strongly in what Sherry Turkle (1984) describes as a "romance" with this "second self." As the site of video games and electronic wonder workers, the computer arouses a fascination that borders on love. Even reluctant writers share the joy of generating words that scroll down a screen in pinpoints of light. Valarie Arms (1983) has seen the same delight among college students. When a colleague remarked that a good set of dittoed prewriting questions could do as much as her newly designed software, she quickly agreed, but added, "I've never had to give a student a second mimeographed sheet because he thought it was fun" (356). What the computer adds is not so much a new cognitive challenge as a new affective pull.

Several teachers in our action research surveyed their students for feelings about writing in general and writing with computers in particular.[1] Whether they used word processing or pen and paper, students reported a whole gamut of emotions: happy, inspired, proud, satisfied, surprised, relieved, angry, confused. We did see a sharp emotional contrast between the profiles of low-skilled and high-skilled writers, no matter what tool they worked with. Just as we have not identified any special "computer mode" of cognitive process, we have not found a single computer mode of affective process.

At the same time, fascination with the computer can spill over into more positive attitudes toward writing. Carrie Henly describes its impact on her lower-skilled high school students:

> I have the highest regard for the power of the computer to build motivation and concentration. . . . Students who could not be counted on to remain seated for ten minutes at a stretch in the regular classroom . . . would sit at the computer and work, often ignoring other students' attempts to distract them, for virtually an entire fifty-five-minute class.

Students in WritingLands express certain feelings so often that I believe writing with computers must make those feelings more common or intense. Writers working with electronic tools more often express *excitement, frustration, interest → fascination,* and *competence* or *incompetence.* These are the affective states teachers need to consider as they design a WritingLand.

For example, we know that children are fascinated by computers, yet they are easily frustrated and threatened by the new skills they must learn to use them. So we start by reducing stress: we give each writer a successful first experience and a printout to show off at home.

Writing and Design

The process of writing is technical and human, private and social, goal-directed and recursive. Perhaps most of all, writing is a process of designing: the writer's task is to invent something that is both "aesthetically pleasing and useful" (Ehrmann and Balestri 1987, 10). As teachers, we also engage in design. We write with our students, of course, but we are often less conscious of our own creativity when we design learning experiences and writing environments, making them "aesthetically pleasing and useful."

The chapters to come look beyond the individual writer to the classrooms of process-oriented teachers. Chapter 6 describes some imaginative lessons that get writers started with word processing. Chapters 7, 8, and 9 show how several teachers design learning experiences that bring together the cognitive, social, and affective processes of writing with computers.

Notes

1. This study was based on the work of Alice Glarden Brand (1987), including her Brand Emotions Scale for Writers. After assisting Brand in refining the BESW, I gave the test to middle school writers and used the BESW classification of emotions to analyze my fieldnotes. See Flinn 1986a, 314–21.

II The Key Variable—
Good Teaching

6 Starting to Teach Writing with Computers

Graduate students in my "Theories of Writing" seminar walk nervously to the lab. Ranging in age from twenty-five to almost fifty, several warn me that they have never touched a computer and will probably "do it all wrong." Laughing, I count them off in pairs, gesture at the computers, and hand each pair a laminated *New Yorker* cartoon featuring two characters. (The keyboards are molded with a ledge that holds a cartoon in full view just below the monitor.) During this activity, *students will carry on a conversation, but they will not talk.* I point silently to the student on the left in each pair, then to the character on the left in the cartoon.

"Okay, you begin. Give yourself a name, type it out ending with a colon, then write what you want your character to say. When you've made your first comment, hit 'RETURN' twice and let your partner type a reply. Keep the dialogue going until I call 'Time', but don't talk!"

Exchanging glances, the characters begin their scripts. Soon giggles start, but the writers remember (or are reminded) to communicate only with the keyboard. They type vigorously, their faces intent with amusement, surprise, or mock revenge. No one is lost for words. Even the computer-shy newcomers pour their energy into getting their points across. I call "Time," giving some of them an extra minute to have the last word. They save and print out two copies of their dialogues. Each pair passes around the cartoon to introduce their characters. (Better still, if the cartoons have been made into transparencies, they can be enlarged on a screen.) The team then performs their script. The session ends with applause and good humor, the initial tension now forgotten.

Don Murray (1985) stresses the importance of using "the first hour of the first day" to set a tone for the writing workshop. The first day with computers can be overwhelming. Too many teachers resort to lessons in computer literacy, hoping that the writing process will follow. We have found that the best way to start is with a real writing experience, making computer instruction as simple, natural, and unobtrusive as we can. Our first lessons tend to have several features in common:

1. They produce short, meaningful pieces of writing.
2. They require revision.
3. They are social or collaborative.
4. They result in quick, informal publication.

Short, Meaningful Writing

Starting with short, easy pieces is far more effective than preteaching the software. Often it is the teacher, not the students, who feels a need for such prior instruction. When a personal computer first arrived at home, I approached the machine like a good adult learner: working the on-screen tutorial, reading and underlining the manual, taking notes. Eventually, I dared to compose a letter. Then my third grader wanted a turn. I showed Mark the shift, delete, and space keys, the four cursors, and the return key for ending a paragraph. In fifteen minutes, he had typed this story about his adventure with a classmate newly arrived from Japan:

> On Valentine's Day Takeshi and I went to his house. He brought out some cartoon books written JAPANESE. We walked in back of his house and climbed over the fence . . .
>
> and we were in the creek. ; So we walked across the water. And we were on the other side of the creek. I felt excited because I never been in a creek before. And I said, "Easy, easy over there." So we walked across the creek again. Takeshi and I stepped in some deep mud and our shoes got stuck.
>
> We only got one shoe out and it felt heavy. So we walked to his house at 6:30 p.m. And my dad came and got me. And I was grounded for one day.
>
> THE END

Older students learn almost as quickly if they too can begin with short, easy pieces. Direct instruction in commands and keyboarding seems to have limited transfer. Joan Thomas's eighth graders began the year with their word processor's tutorial and some practice exercises requiring them to manipulate the cursor, do block movements, and add, delete, and replace text. Then she assigned their first original piece of writing, an essay of several pages portraying a classmate. (This topic had been successful in previous years as a pen-and-paper assignment.) As usual, the class began with interviewing, note taking, and journal writing. Then students were invited to start drafting either at the computers or at their desks. Joan Thomas describes the results:

> My [eighth graders] were willing enough to work through the tutorials and exercises. But by the time I asked them to write a real paper, they were just as startled as if they had never touched a keyboard; in fact, most of them decided to compose by hand. The next year, I scrapped the tutorials and began with short but original pieces of writing. I think you just have to get through that awkwardness at the beginning, and there's no substitute for practice with real writing.

Getting started with short, meaningful texts relieves stress. Peggy Ryan introduces the computer by having children as young as second graders write captions for magazine pictures at the keyboard; each caption is then printed and mounted with the picture for display. Although captions may seem more like an exercise than a real writing experience, their brevity lets a whole class get something in print on the first day, even with minimal access to one or two computers.

To help students complete meaningful texts even in a brief lab period, first do some planning by hand. With guided prewriting experiences, students will arrive at the lab ready to draft. Many writers go blank staring at a blank screen—just as they do at a blank piece of paper. In one urban middle school, Rosalynde Scott and Lois Hart often team-teach their lessons, one working in the computer lab, the other in the writing enrichment classroom. Scott helps students brainstorm a recipe—"Cooking with Words." In the classroom, writers toss out ideas ("cinnamon similes" and "parsley personification") and play with arranging them into verse. Then, in the lab, they draft, revise, and print out their recipe poems. Back in the classroom, they draw oversized figures of grinning chefs, and then glue their printouts onto the aprons. Publication!

In Gateway Writing Project workshops, we often use Gabrielle Rico's (1983) techniques to help adult learners get comfortable at the computer. "Clustering," as Rico calls it, may introduce the new writing tools. I write "computer" on the white board in the lab with a marking pen, ringing the word with an oval. Writers sit at the computer with the word processor booted up. They examine this odd machine with each of their five senses, feeling it, sniffing it, imagining how it might taste. As they brainstorm their impressions, I record them on the board, radiating out from "computer," each word in its own oval. When the energy winds down and the board is scrawled full, it may look like figure 11.

At the keyboard, writers use the clustering as the basis for a short expressive piece about their computer. Often these accounts are humorous; someone introduces the machine in the first person, someone creates a dialogue between the writer and the writing tool, but nobody is at a loss for words.

With writers of any age, we begin with short pieces of real writing, teaching the mechanics of word processing as needed. When writers fill a line, we explain wordwrap; when their time is up, we explain how to save files. We postpone lengthy papers until people show some signs of fluency at the keyboard. Meanwhile, we reassure them that their awkwardness will be temporary. And we show them a payoff to compensate—revision.

Revision

Starting with a piece that demands many changes shows students how the computer can help them manage their writing processes. They see that while they lose some time to slow typing, they save even more time by not recopying their drafts.

I saw this demonstrated when two of Georgia Archibald's sixth graders composed their first stories at the keyboard while four classmates wrote the same assignment by hand. The whole process took three class periods: the first and third for drafting, the second for peer response. During the first twenty-minute session, Josh typed 102 words, Anna 75, and the students working with pen and paper a mean of 140 words. It seemed that the computer was having a disastrous impact on fluency.

But the apparent advantage of handwriting faded quickly, in fact by the time this very first story was revised. The students who wrote by hand spent most of their last session recopying. Their final stories averaged just 144 words. Their classmates at the computer, who revised, added, inserted, but did not recopy, averaged 235 words! I realized that even with minimal computer experience and no typing instruction, students can compose at the keyboard without losing fluency. Their finished products will be at least as fluent as those composed by hand—provided the process does not stop with one draft.

For this reason, freewriting is not a particularly good way to introduce students to word processing, even though it's easy and nonthreatening. It simply does not show writers what the computer can do for them. Freewriting normally means fast, nonstop composing; this can't happen the first time at the keyboard. New users should write easy, nonthreatening pieces, but most of them should present a built-in need for revision.

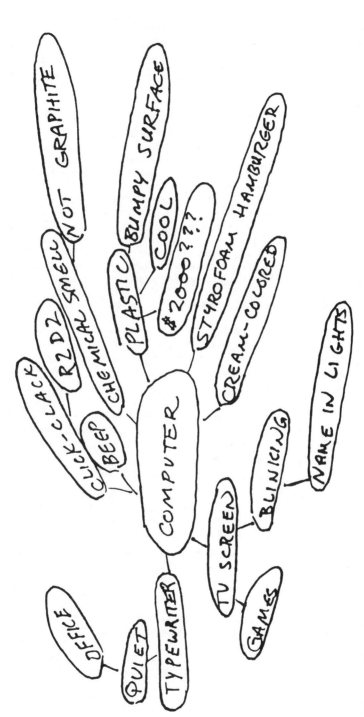

Fig. 11. Clustering on the word "computer."

John Weiss designed a first lesson to showcase the computer's revising power. He brought his twelfth graders to the lab, invited them to pair up at the computers, and handed each team a difficult passage such as the following to read, discuss, and condense to one-fourth the original length:

Précis Assignment: Source Text

Americans are immensely concerned with amusement; but their desire is not so much to amuse themselves as to be amused by someone else. Take music, for instance. Despite a growth in musical appreciation in this century which has been more than considerable, though perhaps it has not been so great as is sometimes supposed, we do not make nearly as much music today as our grandparents did. Instead, we are content to sit back and listen to someone else make music for us. Perhaps we are too lazy to sing and play instruments. Perhaps we are unwilling to go through the discipline necessary to acquire musical facility. Perhaps we are overawed by professional expertness, unaware that much more enjoyment is gained by singing or playing oneself, even though one does it badly, then from hearing it done, however perfectly. Our musical experience is largely receptive, not creative. [147 words][1]

Students talked their way through the précis—deleting, moving, substituting, rearranging until both partners agreed that their version was smooth, succinct, and accurate. Most needed a full class period to finish one heavily-revised paragraph:

Précis Assignment: Responses

Instead of making music as generations have done in the past, Americans today favor listening as a form of amusement. Laziness is one of the main reasons, but also people dont realize the pleasure from playing an instrument. [38 words]

Americans are lazy when dealing with entertainment. they enjoy being entertained more than they enjoy entertaining themselves. For example, although music is enjoyed by many people, few people sing or play an instrument. [33 words]

Although most Americans are highly interested in amusement, especially music, they seem to be lazy in producing it. Thus their idea is to just sit and listen while the young and daring produce it. [34 words]

Amusement is valued highly by Americans, but they are willing to sit back and watch others perform rather than perform themselves. Many people of earlier centuries enjoyed playing musical instruments, but Americans now would rather listen to the professionals. They have lost their ingenuity and have become lazy. [47 words]

John Weiss found that this first experience set the tone for his writing class. Students saw the computer not as a fancy typewriter but as a revision tool.

Collaboration

Collaborative writing is ideal for getting started because it tends to reduce anxiety and increase access. Twenty-four students can pair up in a lab of twelve computers for a full period of précis writing.

The précis can be adapted to other kinds of collaborative summaries. Elementary school writers can pair up at the computer to retell a chapter in their social studies text or outline a process in their science book. The collaboration will lead them to consider more seriously which points are essential, which peripheral, to the message. Secondary or college writers can be given a similar task involving two or three related reading selections; they must find a focus and synthesize material from the readings into a single short commentary.

These writings can be assigned to one, two, or several students. But when the task is collaborative, you can expect to see more revising and more experimentation. When writers collaborate on a single product, they must explain their choices to an audience and discuss alternative choices. The process discourages them from tossing off a quick draft.

Despite these advantages, many writers find it very frustrating to collaborate fully on a single piece. How do writers with incompatible styles share ownership of a text? As a "getting started" activity, true coauthoring seems to work best when the task is brief and not too personal—something either funny or derivative. If cooperative learning is a regular practice in your WritingLand, students will gradually build the trust and the skills in group process to handle more ambitious shared writing projects.

Another style of collaboration is often easier because it does not require students to merge their individual styles. Instead, they write dialogues or scripts which are enhanced by the presence of contrasting voices. The cartoon lesson that began this chapter lends itself to many variations.

I originally saw cartoon dialogues demonstrated by Norma Owen as a junior high lesson in scriptwriting and punctuation—without the computer. Her audience was so delighted with the scripts that several of us adapted the idea for other purposes. In a variation with fourth graders, children pair up at the computers, taking the roles of two characters in a story they've just read, and improvise a dialogue. In another variation, high school students collaborate on dialogue between, for example, a teenager and a mother discussing the price of a designer label shirt. All of these lessons help students start composing freely and enjoyably at the keyboard, even with minimal access.

New writing tools can stretch even further with round-robin composing. Susan Morice takes her college seminar of about ten students to a room with two computers. Each is booted up and the screens reveal the opening paragraph of a little-known story or essay by a well-known author. Two students sit down and compose a second paragraph; then two more take their places and continue the text. When everyone has taken a turn, the groups swap computers and carry the other text to completion. During a break, the instructor makes enough printouts for everyone to read and gives them the original author's version. Writers can then discuss what clues in the opening paragraph led them to develop the text as they did, comparing their approach with that of the author as they do so. It's a lovely lesson in reader response and also a lovely way to get started with computers. The logistics can be adapted to almost any number of students moving from workstation to workstation in a lab.

Clara McCrary uses a very similar lesson with third graders. She types on disk a story from the basal reader, one that the children have complained leaves them hanging. Then she brings students to the lab to compose a better ending. When they have written their response, usually a few sentences, she lets them move one terminal to the right and read a classmate's work, then move once more to read a third version. The group then discusses what they wrote and how they feel about the story with their enhanced endings. Copies are printed to share in the classroom reading collection. Both the process and the product are social, adding to the culture of the WritingLand.

Publication

Most of our best introductory lessons give writers the immediate satisfaction of a "published" copy. Often this simply means a page to tear off the printer and carry home, but the fact of leaving the first composing session with a printout is tremendously reassuring. Teachers can capitalize on this experience.

Joann Hynes teaches in an alternative high school for at-risk students. On the first day, she starts her students writing cinquains. She has them count spaces to arrange the lines in the proper shape and then illustrate the printouts with marking pens. Soon they are ready for more challenging projects.

Back in 1983, after just a few weeks' experience with word processing, Hynes's group of reluctant writers was busy with collaborative research and publication. The project had begun spontaneously as they were discussing problems teenagers face and the difficulty of finding help in a crisis. The students decided to investigate the resources available in their own community. Each one set to work on a different topic—alcoholism, pregnancy, suicide—and entered their findings at the computer. As their data grew, so did their motivation. They felt the list they were creating should be shared with others. The writers paused to create a consistent plan of organization, and when they decided to alphabetize their entries by topic, their teacher showed them how to execute block movements. They continued gathering data, making entries, and going back to supply missing details in earlier entries. When they finished, the school district published their booklet just as they had typed it to distribute in shops and community agencies.

This project shows all four of the features I have been suggesting: each entry is short, yet requires multiple revisions; collaboration makes the task less threatening; the final work is published with pride.

While it is tempting to end this chapter with the success of this collaborative research project, I want to add one warning. Despite our best efforts to make it just a tool, the computer does tend, during the first few weeks, to claim center stage as a novelty. Often it also claims center stage as a nuisance. Your carefully planned lesson is sabotaged by a missing cable. Your new lab aide spends half a class period finding the right disks. Your new software will not boot up.

Relax. Your students may not complete three assignments by mid-October. Your new typists may have more errors in their printouts than you ever recall them having in their handwritten papers. Most of us, whether in grade school or in graduate school, wound up lowering our expectations for a while (shorter papers, looser deadlines, less-perfect proofreading) as we and our students adjusted to new writing tools. Gradually we stopped feeling guilty and learned, day by day, to integrate word processing into our own style of teaching.

Plan the first few experiences at the keyboard as writing sessions, not as computer sessions. Be assured that the losses you see will be temporary. You will be surprised how soon the machine melts into the environment of the WritingLand.

Notes

1. From B. I. Bell. *Crowd Culture*. New York: Harper and Row. Reprinted from J. E. Warriner and F. Griffith. 1965. *English Grammar and Composition*. New York: Harcourt.

7 Teaching "Process" with Structure

Motherhood, apple pie, the American flag, and the writing process. It's almost gotten that bad. Every new writing text, every grammar handbook, claims to be based on *"the* writing process." Look inside the covers, and you'll find something like the "four steps" or the "three stages"—some rigid, linear prescription that contradicts what we now know about the way real writers work.

In the case studies of the last twenty years, researchers such as Janet Emig (1971), Donald Graves (1975), Sondra Perl (1979), and Lucy Calkins (1983) have depicted writing processes that weave back and forth: planning, drafting a few paragraphs, quickly reviewing and revising, looking back to plan a new lead, then perhaps scrapping it all to plan again. Instead of a linear series of steps in the production of a paper, current models show a recursive set of strategies for thinking that come into play again and again as writers work.

When we watch students write, we see that there is not one writing process but many. Highly skilled writers tend to work with the text as a whole; low-skilled writers may have tunnel vision as they concentrate on surface mechanics and lose track of meaning. And the differences do not stop there.

The writing process is as individual as the sleeping process (On your back? On your stomach? Head rested on one elbow?). Our teachers often survey their classes, asking, "When you wrote this essay, how many of you started with an outline? With brainstorming? With some kind of drawing?" As students discuss their own writing processes and compare them with those of their peers, we may add to their data the stories of some professional writers. (Robert Frost believed so strongly in writing great quantities and selecting the best that he required his poetry students to *weigh* their writing portfolios.) Students start paying attention to how they write—to what works for them and what might work better. And they gradually gain the power to manage their own processes.

Yet the new research poses some problems for teachers. Cognitive models of composing tend to blur the distinctions between writing activities. Since plans are revised and revisions are planned and the mind is constantly moving, students may ask, "What difference does it make?" Though the writing process is recursive and individual, our lessons unfold in linear time. Teachers must plan activities with some sort of beginning, middle, and end, following some sort of linear sequence. We must orchestrate the learning of a whole class, even if organized in groups or pairs.

I have come to define the problem in this way: *How do we design "linear" classroom experiences of prewriting, drafting, and editing with feedback that will help students use the "recursive" processes of planning, translating, and reviewing?* What we do in guiding writers through the process is critical. We must create a sort of counterpoint as the linear flow of teaching meets the non-linear, recursive flow of writing and thinking. Table 2 is my attempt at a visual model. The processes of instruction are linear and sequential, though the processes of writing are nonlinear and recursive. What goes on in a lesson is not simply a mirror of what goes on in a writer. So how *should* teachers plan lessons?

When we first began working with the writing process, many of us developed a teaching style reminiscent of the 1960s' "open classrooms" or the British infant schools. We read Ken Macrorie's *Writing to Be Read* (1971) or Peter Elbow's *Writing without Teachers* (1973). We saw ourselves as facilitators, helping writers discover their own processes, choose their own topics, trust their own classmates for feedback, publish their own books, become their own experts. Of course, regardless of how natural it may look, teaching in this way requires a great deal of planning. Behind the scenes there is a subtle structure and discipline that makes possible the freedom of a student-centered classroom.

Yet today, I question whether a nondirective approach really is the ideal. George Hillocks's (1986) massive meta-analysis, a study synthesizing years of experimental research, has caused some of us to rethink and redefine "process" approaches to teaching writing. Along with the nondirective "natural" process, Hillocks identifies an "environmental" process with more active guidance and structure. The studies he reviews suggest that writing improves most in classes where teachers provide support for students to manage their own writing processes: specific ways to revise, alternative techniques for planning, varied modes of discourse. Perhaps the "process approaches" we recommend in the writing projects should be more environmental, more structured. As Calkins (1986) says, "Don't be afraid to teach" (p. 163).

Hillocks's conclusion is not the last word on the subject. In the

Table 2
The Counterpoint of Teaching the Writing Process

	Linear	Recursive

Teacher	organizes activities:
	    prewriting lessons
	    drafting lessons
	    editing lessons
	    peer feedback
	    conferencing
		writes with class:
		    plans
		    translates
		    reviews
		thinks
		relates to students

Student	takes part in
	activities:
	    lessons
	    peer meetings
	    conferences
		writes:
		    plans
		    translates
		    reviews
		thinks
		relates

experiments he reviews, most teachers were randomly selected and didn't have any special training in the writing process. What Hillocks calls a "natural process" may be just a haphazard attempt to let students do their own thing. Since my own first year of teaching was spent in an alternative school where classes were twenty minutes long and often cancelled to feed the goats, I can well imagine that disciplined, well-honed writing is rarely the result. But if the natural process means something like Nancie Atwell's writing workshop (1987), the results can be extraordinary. How "natural" should "process" be?

I am intrigued by the notion of an "environmental process." Most teachers I've observed in the Gateway Writing Project use process approaches to writing which are rather structured, relying both on mini-lessons and on a prepared WritingLand environment. For example, they may teach their peer groups to give helpful feedback with response guides by asking, "How does the writer help you experience what is happening with your five senses? Underline the most vivid details. Find one sentence or description that needs to be more vivid and help the writer revise it." They have specific skills, specific goals, in mind, and they structure their writing workshops accordingly.

Successful, process-oriented teachers may guide writers toward quite distinct goals. Each may design a learning environment with a distinct style. If computers are available, they will support the structure of that particular WritingLand.

The structures we choose have a powerful impact on the way students write and the way they talk about writing. The next two chapters show how four Gateway-trained teachers shape the composing process. I'll describe an experiment that revealed more than I had anticipated about that diverse phenomenon, the "process approach."

8 Harry, the Detective

The teacher is the most important variable in classroom learning. Unfortunately, most educational research has overlooked the teacher to focus instead on methods, or textbooks, or software.

It's not surprising that early studies of writing with computers tended to ask, "Do students produce better writing with the computer or with pen and paper?" (We wouldn't think of asking, "Do students produce better writing with pen or with pencil?") Researchers looked at the computer as the "independent variable," a sort of electronic first cause of whatever students might do. But the inconclusive results of such studies suggest that researchers might best view computers as the "dependent variable" (Michaels 1986) whose impact depends on many factors in the learning environment. What computers do is shaped by each student's and each teacher's customary approach to writing, as well as by each teacher's design for computers in the writing class.

I knew all this, or thought I did, but still I had to try it for myself. In 1984–85, four Gateway Writing Project teachers worked with me on a "quasi-experiment." Two had regular access to computers, and two others provided comparison settings for pen-and-paper composing. A total of fifteen sixth graders wrote with the computer, and forty-six used pen and paper alone. During nine months of collaborative action research, I observed all four teachers frequently. I wrote fieldnotes in their classrooms and interviewed their writers for case studies. Our research took place in the context of normal classroom activities.

Then in February we ran our experiment. We asked all sixty-one students to spend a half hour revising the same short narrative.[1] Despite my emphasis on context, I still felt a lingering hope that the computer itself would make a difference in student writing, that we would find some "computer mode" of revising or editing. So in our well-planned experiment, the only independent variable was the writing tool. And, of course, the writing teacher.

The story the children would rewrite was based on a draft actually written by a student in another class. To develop the task, the sixth-grade teachers had first inventoried the kinds of weaknesses they felt their students should be able to revise, from poor characterization to lack of development to homonym errors. Next I rewrote our story to contain the target weaknesses. We field-tested the assignment by trying the task ourselves and by giving it to students from another school. Then we eliminated a few ambiguous items to produce this classic of detective fiction:

> This is story about Harry, a timid person who is easily scared. One night at midnight, Harry saw some shadows behind the treehouse in the park wich isn't far from the city bank. He couldn't here what they were saying, so he ran for the police because he thogt they might be bankrobbers but he stopped and said to himself, "wait I'll see what they are doing first," then he also said, "forget it, man, Im chicken," and ran for the police once more. When he got back with the police, he found out that his friends were waiting to surprise him. They really wanted it to be a surprise. Cause it was his brithday. Now the time was 1:05 A.M. the exact time he was born.

Our sixth graders were asked to revise "Harry" as a regular in-class assignment. This rather contrived task differed from their usual work of writing and revising original papers. Yet it was not an alien experience. Students had been asked to revise texts from other classes during lessons which focused on specific writing techniques. They also regularly worked in pairs to help other students revise, so they were familiar with the task of critiquing someone else's writing.

I watched in the classroom as each group approached the Harry task with a discussion of "What makes a good story?" The four teachers were remarkably consistent in the way they introduced this discussion. They guided their students to consider content as well as form, and on the board they recorded a list of possible items for revision as the class identified them: "boring lead," "spelling," "bad description."

The pen-and-paper students then received "Harry," typed double-spaced, to mark up and rewrite on lined paper. The computer students called up the text on their monitors, revised, saved, and printed out their revised stories. All students were allowed thirty minutes to complete their revisions. (We had feared that the computer commands would take extra time, but it turned out that the time saved in not recopying the text compensated for that.) On the whole, I believe our procedures were as rigorously controlled as they could be for research conducted in a natural classroom setting.

Before analyzing the data, we typed all the handwritten papers with the same software used by the computer groups. Next we counted the words in each revision to get a *fluency score*. Then two research-team teachers who were not involved in the experiment read each paper for overall quality and a *holistic score*. (We used four points for scoring. A "1" was assigned to the original "Harry" or to revisions that added as many flaws as they corrected. A "4" showed "good development of story" as well as "good editing of mechanics," and the middle scores reflected some combination of skills.)

Finally, we did an *error analysis* to assess revisions of wording, mechanics, and organization. Here are the totals for each target flaw— the number of possible corrections:

mechanics	12
dull or redundant wording	10
fragments and run-ons	2
introduction and conclusion	2

In each story, we checked to see how many of these planted weaknesses the writer merely detected and which were improved or corrected. To "detect" means replacing one dull word with another (*ran* to *went*) or changing a fragment to a different sentence error. To "improve/correct" means repairing a weakness or rewriting to eliminate it. We obtained a score for each writer by recording the number of changes that improve or correct the text as a percent of the target flaws.

The "Harry" task was designed to compare revising with the computer and revising with pen and paper. In fact, the data did reveal some statistically significant differences. The computer students were more fluent in the way they developed the 127-word "Harry" draft: their average length was about 148 words, while the pen-and-paper students averaged 129 words. There were no significant differences in the error analysis, but the computer students earned somewhat higher holistic scores: on a scale of 2 to 8, the computer mean was almost 6.1, while the pen-and-paper mean was less than 5.3.

The performance of the computer students is still more impressive because a fall writing sample used as a pretest shows they started the year with slightly weaker skills than the pen-and-paper groups. The significant results appear in table 3. What a victory for the computer! But was it, really? A closer look at the data made me suspicious. All computer students did not revise in the same way, and neither did all pen-and-paper students. In fact, most of the differences in the scores could be traced to one or another of the four specific classes. A look at the results of the error analysis proved more enlightening still. There were characteristic patterns of revision in each classroom, patterns which did not simply correspond to differences in writing tools. Instead, they corresponded to differences in each teacher's approach to writing, differences I had observed and documented in a year of fieldnotes. It

Table 3
Quality and Fluency of "Harry" Revisions[2]

Measures	Group Means	
	Computer (N = 15)	Pen and Paper (N = 46)
Writing Sample Pretest (2–12 scale)	6.466	6.717
"Harry" Revision Holistic (2–8 scale)	6.067	5.261
Fluency (Original = 127 words)	148.066	129.130

seemed that the key variable might not be writing *tools*, but writing *teachers*.

After the scoring, I was able to interview students in each class who worked with the case study research. They explained why they had made particular revisions in the "Harry" tale. To help computer students recall their own thinking processes, we watched a replay of their composing sessions with COMPTRACE. To help the pen-and-paper students, we looked at their marked-up copy as well as their final rewrite.

These writers' comments confirmed my suspicions about the character of each WritingLand and helped me to define the WritingLand model of "Good Writing." The next chapter will portray these classes in detail. The portraits will show how each teacher uses writing tools to emphasize certain features of good writing, to teach "process" with her own characteristic "structure."

Notes

1. For a detailed discussion of this quasi-experiment, see Flinn 1986a. The "Harry" task is discussed in chapter 4, pp. 123–31, and in chapter 7, pp. 292–308.

2. Data were analyzed with the General Linear Models (GLM) procedure of the Statistical Analysis System (SAS). Using the pretest as a covariant, we found that both fluency and holistic scores on the "Harry" task differed significantly from the computer group to the pen-and-paper group:

Holistic scores: Computer—6.067; Pen & paper—5.261. $F(2, 58) = 4.33$, $p < .05$.

Fluency: Computer—148.066; Pen & paper—129.130. $F(2, 58) = 4.45$, $p < .05$.

9 Three Faces of "Harry"

Four Teachers, Three Models of "Good Writing"

The "Harry" experiment was supposed to compare revising by hand with revising by machine, but I found that the most striking comparisons had little to do with writing tools. In each of the sixth-grade groups, writers changed the story in characteristic ways (table 4).

The three groups were taught by four process-trained teachers, each one a leader in the Gateway Writing Project. Peggy Ryan had the small heterogeneous class with daily computer access. Norma Owen taught a large class of upper-ability students working with pen and paper. The other two teachers worked as a team: Margaret Hasse taught a heterogeneous class using pen and paper; two of her students spent one day each week writing with computers in a gifted program taught by Georgia Archibald.

When I designed the study, I believed these groups to be quite comparable: 4 Writing Project teachers differing by tool used (2 computer, 2 pen and paper) and by class ability (2 mixed, 2 high). But as I examined the data, I saw that each teacher's class seemed to emphasize a different aspect of revision, earning the top scores in that area but not in others. No single class was consistently superior, but each had its own strengths.

Why would students taught by process-oriented teachers perform so differently on this revision task? The pattern cuts across writing tools, since the Hasse/Archibald class included students with and without computer access. And the differences in the error analysis, so clear when we compare classes (table 4), disappear when we simply compare pen-and-paper students with computer students (chapter 8, table 3).

An intriguing pattern took shape as I looked at these statistics again in the light of my fieldnotes. During the months of observing these four teachers, I had noticed three contrasting emphases in instruction: fluency, word choice, and mechanical correctness. Now I saw that each teacher's emphasis matched the changes her students actually made in "Harry" and corresponded to the high scores on the chart. It seems

Table 4
How Students in Three Groups Revised "Harry"[1]

	Class Means		
Teachers	**Ryan** **(N = 13)**	**Hasse/** **Archibald** **(N = 23)**	**Owen** **(N = 25)**
Writing Sample Pretest (2–12 scale)	5.923	6.652	7.040

"Harry"—Error Analysis
   Mechanics
     (N = 12)
	7.346	9.153	10.800

Word Choice (N = 10)	2.039	2.956	2.020
Sentences (N = 2)	1.462	1.260	1.520
Intro/Con (N = 2)	.615	.653	.720

"Harry"—Product
   Holistic
   (2–8 scale)
	5.769	5.653	5.120

Fluency (Draft = 127 words)	150.769	130.739	127.76

that each teacher had guided her students to *see* certain features of writing. These items leapt off the page—or screen—when they saw the short story. Students tended to revise according to a model of "good writing" formed in each classroom community.

The four teachers had emphasized three different aspects of revision. When the data for fluency, word choice, and mechanics were analyzed, the differences in the three groups proved statistically significant. Ryan's class aimed for fluent development; the class working with Hasse and Archibald aimed for vivid word choice; Owen's class aimed for mechanical correctness.

Watch how each of these teachers, with their common training and writing process orientation, managed to design a successful writing workshop with quite different values.

Fluency: "Good Writing Is Well-Developed"

Peggy Ryan's classroom, which included Bob and Mary, has been the focus of chapters 2, 3, and 4. On the September writing sample, her students earned the lowest holistic scores of the three groups. Five months later, working with the computer, their "Harry" revisions slightly surpassed those of their counterparts in holistic scores. The most striking feature of their writing is its fluency; Ryan's students wrote the longest papers—150.8 words—far longer than the 128 and 131 words averaged by the other two groups. This class also showed the weakest editing of mechanics.[2] My fieldnotes describe a pattern of instruction that might lead to this pattern of revision.

Peggy Ryan often urged her writers to develop their papers and experiment freely, putting fluency before correctness. I'd see her pause at a student's desk, read through a draft in progress, and urge, "Tell me more about . . ." or "Give your reader more details." Peer partners echoed her concerns, coaching, "Put in some more description here," or "You need more stuff about. . . ." Students wrote daily either by hand or by machine, so that after a few months of practice the computer did not interfere with their fluency.

Writers in this class also considered spelling and word choice, often working with a dictionary or thesaurus alongside the computer. Yet their teacher did not spend much class time on editing skills. Students rarely produced mechanically perfect papers by the final printout, and Ryan seldom commented on the remaining errors. When I asked about this, she explained that surface correctness was a developmental goal in her class, not a requirement for acceptable daily work. Her primary concern was to help students express their ideas creatively and fluently.

Through the case studies, I have already suggested that Bob and Mary were working from rather consistent models of "good writing." Mary seemed to define good writing as descriptive; Bob seemed to define it in terms of length and spelling. Taking a broader view of Ryan's class, I want to suggest that the entire writing community had been guided by an implicit model of good writing: fluency or development. This model, created by the teacher, interacted with and reshaped each child's personal model of good writing. The result was a WritingLand of many individuals with many variations on a common theme.

Remember Bob's comment on "Harry"? "This wasn't too long of a story. I think that at the end he . . . should have wrote a little bit more instead of ending it so quickly." He was also quite delighted when his triple-spaced "Spy Hunter" printed out as four whole pages. Mary's version of the fluency model was more sophisticated—she looked for descriptive detail rather than length for its own sake. Yet her approach to description was mainly additive: "I added two more adjectives to make it more descriptive," she said of her myth, referring to "horrible" and "wonderful." Bob and Mary, like most of Peggy Ryan's students, tended to revise by developing.

See how Gary, a student with average skills, developed "Harry." With 156 words and a holistic score of 6, Gary's revision could well represent the class mean:

> This is story about Harry, a timid person who is easily frightened. One dark gloomy night, Harry saw some shadows behind the treehouse. That isn't far from the city bank. He couldn't here what they were saying, so he ran for the police. He thought they might be bankrobbers but he stopped and said to himself, "wait I'll see what they are doing first."
>
> Then he remembered that they might have guns. So he ran for the police once more. When he got back with the police, he found out that his friends were waiting to surprise him. They really wanted it to be a surprise, because it was his brithday. Now the time was 1:05 A.M. the exact time he was born. They had a very big party that night for Harry. He had got many things for his birthday and he was excited. He had a very good time. He also was suprised!!!!!!

Gary added a few adjectives ("dark," "gloomy"), developed the plot ("they might have guns"), and supplied a conclusion. What he lacked in concrete detail, he made up for in punctuation. Like most of his classmates, Gary approached revision as if the key to good writing were fluency and development.

Vocabulary: "Good Writing Has Interesting Words"

Margaret Hasse and Georgia Archibald worked in the same middle-income, racially mixed, suburban public school. Ever since Archibald's student teaching a decade earlier, they had enjoyed collaborating on lessons, teacher research, and the Gateway Writing Project. They had originated a school publishing center to bind and display children's work.

Hasse created a rich learning environment where a typical question might be, "Which is happier, a paper clip or Scotch tape?" (And a typical student answer might be, "A paper clip because it could be clipped on secret papers and sent to different parts of the world and know all that spy stuff.")

Her classroom was crowded with chair-desks arranged in the usual rows but easy to pivot into pairs and groups. Bookcases lined the two long walls and jutted out into the aisles. A closer look at her bookshelves shows that much of the material was student-authored. Up front near the chalkboard and teacher's desk sat a long table where groups of twelve children could meet for book talks. The atmosphere was somewhat more structured than in Ryan's class (partly because space was not organized in centers), but the approach to the writing process was quite similar.

Hasse did not take part in the Gateway computer institute (due, she admitted, to a fear of technology), but she was a leader in projects ranging from aesthetic education to writing assessment. During my year of observation, her teaching log bubbled with details of her "talented students" and quotes from their writing.

Two students from Hasse's class were chosen to spend one day a week with Archibald in the gifted resource center. Housed in a converted home economics classroom, the center was cluttered with laminated tables, sinks, and animal habitats. A white rat named Mooch peered over the edge of his tank as children untangled verbal codes and practiced for the "Future Problem-Solving Tournament." In this environment, the pace was fast, the curriculum challenging, the students and faculty enthusiastic.

Georgia Archibald had never touched a computer until attending the summer institute, but she was eager to learn with her students. Computers, on a rolling cart, or in the school's well-equipped new lab, became an integral part of her language arts program.

When children from this middle school revised "Harry," some by hand, others by machine, they homed in on the dull and redundant word choice. Of 10 such target words, Hasse's twenty-one pen-and-paper students improved an average of 2.86; her two gifted students who also worked on the computers with Archibald improved 3 and 5 respectively. This makes a combined group mean of almost 3 successful word choice changes, in contrast to about 2 words per student in the other classes.[3] The fieldnotes show how these two teachers guided their writers to form such a model of "good writing."

Hasse stressed finding just the right words to capture a feeling, image, or concept. During the first week of school, she introduced the process of writing and rewriting. She wrote with her students, joking about how messy her draft was becoming as she revised. I watched her move about the room, then pause at one desk. "Look at this!" She waved a girl's paper before the class. "See all the words crossed out? Do you know what that tells me? [Very slowly, with emphasis] Elizabeth is *thinking*!" What a lovely contrast to the way revision is often taught, by praising the neat final product without showing the messy thinking that precedes it. Hasse taught vocabulary directly, but unconventionally. For example, students debated whether someone who fell into *mire* would "drown" or "stick" or "suffocate." Their teacher would often read aloud sentences with overused words in an exaggeratedly bored voice, asking the class to brainstorm some better choices.

Similarly, Archibald often pointed out "wimpy words" and their enriched counterparts, such as "vitamin verbs." Early in the year, her students explored the special vocabulary of computers. They collaborated on a dictionary of terms, each illustrated with a definition and an amusing simile or metaphor ("A disk drive is like a hungry mouth feeding on diskettes" or "A microchip is like a policeman directing electronic circuits").[4]

Here is how Josh, one of the talented writers who worked with both these teachers, applied their lessons to his revision of "Harry." Note that his total length, 100 words, was the shortest of the 61 papers in the study, yet it earned a top holistic score of 8. Clearly his concept of revision is based on something other than fluency:

> This is story about Harry Blake, a timid person that is easily frightned.
> One night at midnight, Harry noticed creepy shadows behind the treehouse in the park. Bank robbers, he thought. He tip-toed in closer to hear what they were saying when he stumbled on a twig.
> "What was that?" Harry raced to the police station.
> When he got back with the police, he found out that his friends were waiting to surprise him. They really wanted it to be a surprise. It was his brithday. Now the time was 1:05 A.M., the exact time he was born.
> "Happy birthday!"

When we replayed his session with COMPTRACE, I asked Josh why he changed *ran* to *raced*. He explained, "Well, I was trying to put some more action into it. You know, *ran* [scowl]. 'The boy ran down the street' [bored, sing-song intonation]. Now, 'The boy *jetted* down the street! [enthusiastic tone]—as Mrs. Hasse would say." (Having heard that lesson in the original, I could appreciate his rendition.) Josh replaced many other bland words: *creepy shadows* for *some shadows*, *stumbled* for *stepped*, *tip-toed* for *moved*, *noticed* for *saw*.

While Josh achieved an unusually strong revision, the average students in the group working with Hasse and Archibald also made effective changes from dull, overused words to precise vocabulary.

Mechanics: "Good Writing Is Correct"

Norma Owen's classroom, serving the upper half of the sixth grade in her suburban middle school, was bright with hanging plants, student posters, and shoebox dioramas. Her curriculum challenged students to read and write through a variety of projects in the content areas.

For a study of aging, each child interviewed an elderly relative, created a story around an aged character, and wrote letters to a resident of a nursing home. For Halloween, partners wrote and answered "Dear Dracula" letters of ghoulish advice. I was struck by the sophisticated thinking and writing in this class. Teams of students worked through packets of natural history articles to design questions corresponding to each level of Bloom's Taxonomy; then each team met with another to trade questions.

Like her counterparts, Owen was a leader in the Gateway Writing Project as well as in curriculum and evaluation projects. She had not attended the computer institute because her school didn't have a lab yet. But she was excited about computers, so she took classes in word processing and database applications to get started on her own.

When this class revised "Harry," their papers showed the strongest editing skills. The average student corrected an impressive 10.8 of the 12 planted mechanical errors and 1.5 of the 2 sentence errors. Yet they also showed the lowest fluency, developing hardly any additional content or detail, and the weakest holistic scores.[5] The fieldnotes explain the pattern of instruction leading to these puzzling results.

Far more than her three colleagues, Owen gave direct instruction in editing. She did not stop with out-of-context grammar exercises, which rarely transfer to actual writing. Instead, she taught students to correct their own writing—individually, and with peer partners.

While such instruction continued all year, this class happened to be involved in a journalism unit during the few weeks just preceding the "Harry" task. Owen handed each writer a fine-line orange "editing pen" and taught them to use proofreading symbols when preparing final copy. They also practiced editing sample papers for wordiness and redundancy, since reporters need to state the facts clearly in as few words as possible. (No wonder these students scored low in fluency!)

When I watched Norma Owen introduce "Harry," I saw the impact of her recent editing lessons. Like the other teachers, she began by asking, "What makes a good story? What sorts of things would you look for in revising a story?" Hands shot up. "Run-on sentences!" "Punctuation!" "Unnecessary words!" the children volunteered. "Yes," agreed their teacher, but then she explicitly coached them to remember characterization, setting, plot, and word choice. She recorded the whole list on the board. "Change it any way you can to make a good story. . . . *You* are the editor."

Students promptly set to work with their orange editing pens and proofreading symbols, attacking the errors with concentration and authority. Ignoring their teacher's suggestions, they approached "Harry" just as they had so many recent news editing samples.

Their response might have been different in October, right after creating "Dear Dracula" letters. But in February, after their journalism project, the aspect of "good writing" uppermost in their minds was correctness. This emphasis seemed to distract them from more substantive revisions, lowering the holistic and fluency scores in an otherwise very capable group of writers.

Look, for example, at how Luke edited "Harry." He fixed 11 of the 12 mechanical errors and improved the sentence structure, but left most of the text unchanged. His revision earned a holistic score of 6 on a 2–8 scale:

> This is a story about Harry Jones, a person who is easily scared and can't really make desicions. He is around ten or eleven years old.
>
> One night at midnight, he saw some shadows behind the treehouse in the park, which isn't far from the City Bank. He couldn't hear what they were saying, so he ran to the police because he thought they might be bankrobbers. All of a sudden he stopped and said to himself "Wait a minute, I'm going to see what they are doing first," then he said "Forget it man, I'm scared," and ran for the police again. When he returned with the police, he found out that his friends were waiting to suprise him. They really wanted it to be a suprise because it was his birthday. Now it was 1:05 in the morning the exact time he was born.

When I asked for his diagnosis of the original draft, Luke stressed the surface problems: "The first time I read it, *thogt* and *brithday* jumped right out at me. The second time I noticed the other spelling mistakes." He also reworked the lead to fit Harry's character, explaining that Harry goes for the police, then stops, and finally decides to go after all. But he largely ignored the dull and redundant words and did little to develop the story.

Most of Luke's classmates dealt with "Harry" in much the same way, marking editing symbols deftly on the printed text, then recopying in ink. Sometimes they tightened a phrase or two, but their focus was mainly on proofreading. Since I watched for nine months as Norma Owen guided this class through various writing processes, I know that these students normally revised for content, style, and a whole range of other concerns. But the chance juxtaposition of "Harry" with the editing lessons led them to act as if their ideal of "good writing" were merely correct mechanics.

Teaching the "Writing Process"

Given the same task and directions, four groups of students revised in three different patterns. Those patterns, in turn, can be traced to the instructional emphases of their teachers as observed in their classrooms. Effective writing teachers guide their students to *see* a text with new eyes. I've said that the computer is "programmed" by the writer; it seems that the taste of a classroom writing community is "programmed" by the teacher.

Our findings have some important implications for process approaches to teaching writing. Consider what students have to learn before they can deal with revision at all.

Dewey (1967 [1916], 80) defines education as the "continuous reconstruction of experience." Britton (1970, 15) speaks of a "world representation" distilled from experience which shapes the learner's view of new experiences and is itself reshaped. When students revise, they must first "resee" a text in the light of some internalized representation of "good writing," then reconstruct the text, then look again to see if the new text fits their representation.

Writers who cannot revise seem to be stuck in the bondage of their own first drafts. As Frank Smith (1982) explains, they must learn to step back from what they have written and change roles from author to editor. Then they can see the gap between their meaning and their texts, and reconstruct the text accordingly.

Research has shown that most students—whether or not they use computers—simply don't know how to revise. When asked to improve a text, they make only superficial corrections, and often do a poor job at that.

Look at the data from the National Assessment of Educational Progress, based on handwritten papers by thousands of nine-, thirteen-, and seventeen-year-olds, most with teachers untrained in process approaches to writing. According to the latest NAEP survey (November 1986), nearly all students say they revise by correcting spelling and punctuation; about two-thirds report changing words or adding information, and about half report deleting material; few revise by moving larger units or rewriting extensively. NAEP suspects the real picture is bleaker, since students may say they use such strategies as revising or planning without knowing how to use them well. The study concludes, "Teachers need to help students understand these processes more fully and manage them more effectively" (73).

In the Harvard Microcomputer and Literacy Project (Michaels 1986), months of observing in two sixth-grade classrooms led to similar findings. The researchers hoped that placing computers in two writing classrooms would promote more revising and more peer dialogue about writing, but they found little of either. As in NAEP, the teachers had minimal training in teaching writing. In fact, the Harvard teachers used the following rather odd version of the "process approach":

1. Students wrote first drafts by hand.
2. Teachers red-marked all the errors.
3. Each student typed and printed a correct copy.[6]

With such a program, it's no surprise that few children discovered they could use the computer to resee their texts, to reconstruct their meanings.

Yet in the classrooms taught by all four of our teachers, we found sixth graders quite capable of revision. Not only could they revise, but they revised in specific ways, following a model of "good writing" they had learned from their teachers. Clearly, revision can be taught—by hand and by computer. This chapter has described some of the writing experiences in each class that helped students internalize and apply a model of revision.

The computer is not an isolated variable, but a flexible writing tool. It does not favor any particular kind of revision. Word processing makes it physically easier for students to revise toward any and all of the three goals:

> *Fluency*—A writer can insert new material at any point in the text.
>
> *Word Choice*—A writer can delete, add, or substitute words for flavor and precision.
>
> *Mechanics*—A writer can repeatedly correct surface errors and polish form without introducing new errors in recopying.

Why limit ourselves to one of these models of revision? Why not teach students to revise for fluency *and* word choice *and* mechanics? Of course. Our four teachers would insist, accurately, that they *do* teach all "faces" of revision. (Remember that when planning this study we assumed that these four Writing Project leaders shared the same process approach to teaching writing. From observations in their classes, I saw each of them guiding students through multiple drafts, coaching revision at all levels. The three faces of "Harry," striking as they are, reflect variations on a single approach, not three different approaches.)

Then again, why should all students in a class learn to value *my* model of good writing? Shouldn't a teacher help students develop their own individual tastes? (In the course of the year, as students learned a language to talk about their choices, this is exactly what happened. Bob and Mary and many others acquired personal models of "good writing" to explain what they liked or disliked in a text.)

As a writing teacher, I often feel like an orchestra leader or a football coach. We help our students play their own instruments, their own positions. We encourage each one to experiment, to practice, to try out roles and strategies and interpretations. We nurture their individual voices.

But whether or not we want to, if we teach effectively we are going to wave our batons and direct our writers. We are going to bring them together to produce a symphony, a touchdown, a collaborative publication. And much as we respect each writer's differences, we'll leave our own mark on the writing community. Good teaching is the most powerful "program" we can run—on any writing tool.

So in each WritingLand, I suspect there will be a shared, often implicit, model of "good writing." At the same time, each student will develop his or her own sense of "good writing," one that is unique yet responds to the beat of the class.

Notes

1. Data from the "Harry" task were analyzed for instructional emphases with the General Linear Models (GLM) procedure of the Statistical Analysis System (SAS), with significance set at .05. All three proved to be significant. A detailed discussion appears in Flinn 1986a.

2. Ryan taught small groups of 15 to 23 students in sixth-, seventh-, and eighth-grade classes. Among the 15 sixth graders, full data are available for 13; their statistics appear in table 4.

Using the pretest as a covariant, Ryan's class differed significantly from the others in fluency (word count): $F(2, 58) = 11.47$, $p < .05$.

3. Hasse's class of 23 includes the 2 students who worked on the computers with Archibald. Using the pretest as a covariant, this group differed significantly from the others in revision of dull or redundant words: $F(2, 58) = 4.36, p < .05$.

4. The statistics in this chapter include only 2 of Archibald's students, the ones drawn from Hasse's classroom. But if we run the analysis using all 7 students in the gifted program, we see the same emphasis on word choice. Scores for Archibald's whole group on the Harry task:

Mechanics	9.929
Word Choice	3.714
Sentences	1.143
Intro/Con	1.143
Fluency	178.142
Holistic	6.857

Unfortunately, there are no pretest scores for Archibald's five students who were not involved in the action research. But if we estimate their pretest scores by those of the two students we have, the results are just as striking: considering all 28 students who worked with Hasse and Archibald, word choice is the significant revision emphasis: $F(2, 63) = 5.67, p < .05$.

5. Using the pretest as a covariant, Owen's class of 25 differed significantly from the others in correcting the planted surface errors: $F(2, 58) = 14.51, p < .05$.

6. This explanation of the approach to "the writing process" in their classrooms was presented by the two teachers working with the Harvard Microcomputer and Literacy Project at the 1986 Ethnography in Education Research Forum, University of Pennsylvania, April 1986.

III Designing
WritingLands

10 Maps to the Territory

Somehow in my mind I still picture the "Writer" as someone who sits alone in an attic, pondering and scribbling—or like Thoreau in a cabin, observing and writing in a journal. I'm not sure those solitary authors were ever the norm. In *Room of One's Own,* Virginia Woolf explains that most nineteenth-century women novelists did their writing in the family sitting room, amid interruptions from children, husbands, and chores. By contrast, a recent survey of academic writers (Bernhardt and Appleby 1985) shows that today's professional writing tends to be collaborative, the product of team research, peer feedback, or joint authorship.

In any case, writing with a computer in school is almost inevitably social. Instead of covering the scribbled lines with a palm, the writer must display even the first tentative draft in lighted print on a screen open to passersby. By making the writing process public and the written products instantly publishable, the new tools intensify the social nature of composing. School writers can seldom get access to a computer on demand, when inspiration strikes; their writing is subject to the constraints of lab schedules, technical aid, and software supply.

Managing this physical and social environment is crucial in teaching writing with computers. Yet few teachers are prepared for this role. Even when they know how to manage a classroom writing workshop, they may be frustrated to find that computers bring more complications and less personal control over them. I've argued that the computer is "programmed" by the writing community that's guided by the teacher. This metaphor suggests that teaching with computers means handling new kinds of power. But in the beginning a more apt metaphor might be "teaching with computers is getting lost in a strange land without a map."

The next chapters will focus on specific features in the design of WritingLands: time and access (chapter 11), space and layout (chapter 12), hardware and software (chapter 13), teachers (14), and peers (15). This chapter will show these elements working together in some successful but contrasting environments, with a look behind the scenes to the planning process that made these WritingLands work.

The writing lab at Hazelwood West High School has been named a Center of Excellence by the National Council of Teachers of English. Starting with a half-sized classroom and two computers, the writing lab has grown to a suite that includes a tutorial center, a computer-writing classroom, and a large lab serving all subject areas. It is staffed by two English teachers, each for half the day, and a full-time aide.

The school district initially funded the lab for individual work with students. To avoid a negative or remedial image, Anne Wright and her colleagues advertised help with college applications, writing contest entries, and research assignments, as well as with writer's block and standard usage. The first year, computers were used mainly by the lab teachers for record keeping and by faculty in general for preparing lessons. But as individual students tried word processing, teachers noticed they were willing to spend more time experimenting with style and struggling through problems with organization. The staff requested more machines and eventually the writing lab moved to expanded quarters adjacent to the school's library and computer lab.

Now a teacher can bring a whole class to the computer classroom and guide them through some planning or sentence combining techniques. Most students then move on to the lab with their disks to continue writing while their teacher holds individual conferences in the tutorial center. Activities flow easily among the three rooms, and classroom teachers have the support of the lab director and aide at all times.

This setting is very flexible and efficient. If the three areas were not contiguous, it would take many more staff to provide the same level of support for writers. And yet there is enough separation to allow conferencing, whole class instruction, and quiet individual writing to happen at the same time.

Highcroft Elementary, which serves an affluent suburban community, offers a very welcoming school environment. Carpeted throughout, the semi-open spaces are broken by curving walls, steps, and contrasting colors. An antique desk in the principal's office and wood and fabric collectables on the walls bring softness and warmth to the modern architecture.

Once a week, children in grades 5 and 6 march from their cozy language arts room with the rocking chair in the corner through galleries of student artwork to a narrow little lab housing fourteen Apples linked with A-B switches to six printers. Since the computers can accommodate just half the students, two writers normally share a single keyboard. In this WritingLand, computers are used to motivate a wide range of writers—those labeled "gifted" as well as "learning disabled" or "behavior disordered."

In addition to her Gateway training, Rochelle Ferdman has studied with Lucy Calkins and Nancy Atwell. She starts the process in her classroom with a mini-lesson introducing a specific writing technique. She asks everyone to try this in their writing journals, but after the group experience they are free to pursue other ideas. She finds that even reluctant writers can take control of their own processes—choosing whether to do brainstorming, outlining, or clustering to plan a paper.

Next she brings the group to the lab, where the mini-lesson is followed by about forty minutes of paired writing. Later, in the classroom and again in the lab, she guides her writers through structured revision strategies. The sequence concludes with group sharing: one child sits in the big "author's chair" to read as the class gathers on the carpet to listen and respond.

Viewed from outside, Langston Middle School is a flat-roofed, rather nondescript building in a run-down neighborhood of St. Louis. Walking through the doors, the visitor is startled by the bright decor which is accented by children's art and the upbeat stress on academics. Two writing enrichment labs, each staffed full-time by a certified English teacher and an aide, were developed some years ago as part of a citywide program of desegregation and school improvement. When the district bought microcomputers, Langston chose to place them in the Enrichment Lab.

At first, the two labs shared just six computers, placed on rolling carts which could be grouped or separated as needed. Jacqueline Collier, the lead teacher, discovered that computers meshed neatly with the procedures she was already using in her writing program. Since up to forty-five students were scheduled into the lab for blocks of one to two hours, Collier was used to dividing long blocks of time into several activities and large classes of students into small groups. This teaching style helped her make maximum use of minimal access.

Six writers could take turns at the computer, then go directly to one of the tables for peer meetings or to their teacher for conferences. Students collaborated on a creative writing magazine, using graphics software for illustrations, and produced a newspaper with one of the text-and-graphics programs.

When the School Partnership Program brought two public relations executives to Langston, students organized a campaign to promote their school and increase parent involvement. Drawn by computer-printed announcements of the PTO open house, dozens of parents visited the lab. I was impressed with what happened that night. Parents viewed demonstrations of word processing and displays of printed essays and poems. With the help of student tutors, many tried typing out short messages to their children. The boundaries of this WritingLand stretch beyond the lab, beyond the school, and into the urban community.

Orchard Farm, a small rural district in the Missouri River bottomland, seems worlds away from Langston. But when Orchard Farm asked the Gateway Writing Project for help in planning their program, we suggested sending a committee of teachers and administrators to the labs at Langston, Hazelwood West, and other model settings. Borrowing ideas from each site, the Orchard Farm team developed a long-range plan: they would start by sponsoring an inservice program for all English faculty and revising the district's curriculum to stress process approaches to writing. Gradually, they would integrate computers into that curriculum.

Betty Barro's middle school WritingLand is unconventional, but it works. Since her administrators did not want to lose a classroom to create a lab, they set fifteen computers on desk-height rolling carts and placed one with each teacher. When a class does a project, several computers—or all fifteen—can be borrowed and gathered together in one classroom.

This arrangement is very flexible, allowing individual teachers to vary their access and to use computers in their own classrooms. Barro reports that it has become inconvenient, though, as more and more teachers compete for the machines. "We have computers rolling up and down the halls all day," she says, adding that the faculty hopes to gather the computers into a writing lab soon.

Along with Hazelwood West, Pattonville High School has one of St. Louis's pioneer writing centers (Brooks 1989). It was conceived by Susan Morice as a tutorial facility where students could get the individual feedback on papers that is hard to schedule in a secondary school. By the time funding was approved, Pattonville also acquired computers, and the two concepts merged under the supervision of a single teacher.

Today, the English department staffs the writing center by releasing one faculty member each period of the day. Recently Pattonville began keeping the center open for an hour after school so that students can continue working on papers and meet deadlines. Director Barbara

Brooks says, "Even though most students might just need to finish their typing, we felt the supervisor must be an English teacher, someone who could help with the writing, not just with the machines."

A special feature of the program is the use of peer writing tutors. Training is simple. All students learn peer editing and coaching in their junior composition course. Seniors who have enough credits to graduate can elect to be peer writing tutors for one period per day. Barb Brooks explains, "Working as a peer writing tutor is an asset on college applications. We've had graduates coming back to tell us how helpful the experience has been to them."

Peer tutors give many kinds of help. The lab is all one big room, with no private space for conferencing and frequent interruptions. Nonetheless teachers find that the staff of peer tutors means more instructional support and less confusion. Much of the help is informal: "I'm ready to print, can you look it over first?" Tutors may also go into classrooms to explain note taking to small groups and accompany students to the library.

Pattonville's center, with its rotating staff and peer support, provides for very efficient use of resources. It is a "map" to the territory that many secondary schools are choosing to follow.

In the schools I've been describing, computers tend to be integrated into some sort of lab. In other schools, computers have found their way into the library. Lillian Atchison, the librarian at University City High School, developed a tiny computer alcove into a lab that meets very effectively the needs of writers. A dozen computers are arranged on desks along the walls, with an island created in the middle. The librarian's desk is situated just inside the lab, so that she can admit students from the library and send writers back out to read or review their drafts.

This environment solves the dilemma of the writing teacher with twenty-five students and access to a lab of only twelve computers down the hall. Here, a teacher simply reserves the lab and brings the whole class to the library with writing or reading assignments. Teacher and librarian are available to help in the lab during the writing process. Students in the library can work independently or seek help with their research from other staff.

The library added longer hours so that students who don't have computers at home can meet their teachers' deadlines for papers. Atchison comes to school early, and her assistant leaves late. So without increasing staff, the library's computer center can stay open from 7 a.m. to 5 p.m.

The English department now also has a tutorial writing center staffed with one certified teacher each hour and equipped with six computers. This center uses a small third-floor room far from the library. But as partners, the two facilities offer the personal help, the skilled support, and the access to tools that constitute a WritingLand.

One other pre-existing structure seems to offer a natural setting for computers: the publishing center. Founded in many elementary schools to promote student-authored books, these centers have taken advantage of word processing, graphics programs, and more sophisticated desktop publishing software.

Jackson Park School Publishing Center has long been active in University City's "Young Authors' Conference." Each spring, hundreds of children display books they have written, illustrated, and published in bindings of wallpaper, cloth, or plastic laminate. Similar publishing centers are housed in small classrooms at each of the district's elementary schools and are staffed by parent volunteers and part-time aides.

A teacher sends one or two children to the center with penciled drafts, and the staff helps with revising and illustrating. I am familiar with this program not only as a researcher, but also as a parent. When my own children were at Jackson Park, I volunteered as an aide in the publishing center. At that time, parents often typed the final drafts to make the books look more professional; now students revise directly on the computers.

When a dozen computers first arrived, principal Deb Holmes resisted the temptation to place them in a math resource room. Instead, she expanded the publishing center to house the computers. Although these machines were used for all subjects, they became linked with writing because of their location.

Today the publishing process remains simple. The center keeps a stock of blank pages, which have been stitched together in varying thicknesses by parents at home with sewing machines. Children plan out their pages as they design their illustrations. Then they go back to the computer file and use the "Return" key to separate the text that will be printed on each page. The parent volunteer helps with revising and editing, as well as with the computers (having a fresh ribbon ready for the final printing). The text is cut apart and set on each illustrated page with a glue stick. Finally, the booklets are pasted into cardboard-backed covers.

A display of student-authored books, whether typed or handwritten, is impressive. The computer just makes the finished product a bit more professional—and easier for children with poor spelling or handwriting to achieve.

———————

Most of the settings we've seen began as writing programs, which added computers later on. Recently, of course, other schools have used these programs as maps to their own WritingLands. But it is significant that our most successful early sites were writing or reading or publishing centers first, computer centers later. Chris Madigan (1984) uses Piaget's concepts of *accommodation* and *assimilation* to explain why.

When new technology first appears, we "assimilate" it into some category we already know: the car is a "horseless carriage"; the fridge is an electric "icebox." And the word processor is a correcting typewriter. Only after we've gotten some experience with the equipment, do we find ourselves "accommodating," redefining our categories to take advantage of the new machine: the food processor becomes more than an electric beater, the curling iron creates styles that could never come from rollers. And the computer, after serving as a fancy typewriter, takes on new tasks (block functions, boilerplate letters, flexible outlines, and desktop publishing) beyond the capacity of traditional hand tools (Madigan 1984, 144–47).

In the same way, writing teachers first see the lab as a writing center or a publishing house—with computers. Only after working for a time with these familiar categories do we see that the technology has the potential to do more.

I think it's important to notice from where we derive our maps to computer-equipped writing programs. Many schools assimilate to a particularly different map—to the computer lab in the math or business department—and perhaps unwittingly send their writers down some dead-end routes. On the other hand, if we assimilate to a tutorial writing center or publishing program, we'll be following a map to the right territory.

Later, we can revise our map and, in doing so, accommodate the computer. We can find new applications (databases, teleconferencing) and new teaching styles (student lab assistants, flexible deadlines). But in designing a WritingLand, start off with a map of a good, process-oriented writing program.

11 Time and Access to Tools

It's hard to imagine a conventional classroom where pencils are available only once a week. Yet, in many labs, this is the reality of word processing. Again, it's hard to imagine a school where students don't have access to their own notebooks. However, many schools still expect a whole class to save their drafts on a single file disk which can be used only at scheduled times.

Most of the teachers I've observed make deliberate changes in planning and timing to compensate for such technological annoyances. At first they find teaching with computers to be awkward, artificial, the very opposite of the flexible, open style they know from their writing workshops. But gradually, they learn to plan activities that flow smoothly from classroom to lab and back again. Often they recognize the need for such changes only after some funny or tragic mishap of timing.

Consider what happened to nine-year-old Becky one Friday in October, when half of the twenty-four children in her class were introduced to their new lab.

The computer teacher sat each child at one of the twelve computers. Using a peer teaching strategy, she showed them how to load the word processing program so that each child would boot the program, hand the disk to a neighbor, and coach the same process. I was impressed with how smoothly it all went. Then the children were prompted to call up a text file.

Behind this lesson was a great deal of "invisible" planning. The day before, the lab teacher had stayed after school with the children's classroom teacher, Clara McCrary. They talked through the lesson plan. McCrary prepared a text file for the lab teacher, knowing that she herself could not be present while the students were composing at the keyboard. The writing teacher would stay in the classroom with her other twelve students, trusting the lab and the lesson to the computer teacher.

On the disk, McCrary had typed Aesop's fable about the injured lion who at last is willing to accept and to give help. The children called up the file. Quickly recognizing the story from their readers, they noticed that it was "messed up." The lab teachers showed them how to use the block functions to unscramble and move the paragraphs. Then she introduced the writing.

"Your teacher told me you thought this story left you hanging at the end." They nodded. "Well now you can use the computer to give the author some help. Move your cursor to the last line, hit 'RETURN', and add whatever words you want so the ending will be better." Twelve children typed slowly but with concentration until the hour was nearly over. Then the lab teacher invited volunteers to share their writing.

Finally it was Becky's turn. The most sophisticated writer in the class, she had written several sentences and read them aloud with expression. Suddenly the bell rang. "But I'm not done!" she protested. "I've got lots more story to write."

"That's Okay," came the cheerful reply. "You can finish it when your group comes back to the computers—the Friday after next." Becky, looking somewhat bewildered, left her lion moping in his den with a hurt paw until she could return to the lab two weeks later!

As Becky's writing teacher, Clara McCrary realized that no amount of planning could replace her own presence during the composing process. She would have to be on the scene to validate the writing and to make ad hoc decisions about priorities.

McCrary solved the dilemma the next week by accompanying all twenty-four children to the lab herself. A dozen third graders sat on the floor under a row of windows, writing in their journals while she worked with them at the computers. She knew that her support and participation in the writing process were worth some inconvenience.

Let's consider several other problems with computer time and access, and offer some solutions—most of them less drastic than this one.

At Lindbergh High School, one huge lab can easily hold entire classes. But it's the only computer facility serving all subject areas, so teachers must reserve it months in advance.

When the English department began to plan a new writing program, they had to decide whether lab access would be based on competition or teamwork. And when they decided on teamwork, they still needed to plan a schedule that made the best use of what access they had. Their first notion was to allot each class one period per month in the lab—but then they reconsidered.

Lindbergh's writing teachers knew how to guide students through the processes of writing. They valued multiple drafting, feedback, time for reseeing as well as recopying. What good was a single class hour in developing an essay of several pages? Students would almost certainly use most of their time just typing their text. They would never get to the point where they could play with revisions and mull over their options.

So the department decided to allot each class four periods per semester, and most teachers chose to concentrate that access time into a period of about two weeks. This way, students could develop an entire paper, using the computer at several points in the process. On the days when they couldn't reach the lab, they would have time to plan in a journal, review a printout, conference with peers and teacher, or read other assignments. But the four scheduled sessions would give them enough access to work through at least one paper without pressure.

We faced a different problem with lab access during Gateway's summer institute. In 1984, our first year with computers, we were scheduled in two rooms, a writing classroom with movable chair-desks, and a computer lab down the hall with machines jammed in straight rows. The physical and temporal setting told teachers that the Writing Project (a.m.) and the computer course (p.m.) were separate entities, a message that contradicted our goal: an integrated experience of writing with computers. We tried to make connections—discussing planning in the morning, then doing some planning strategies at the keyboard in the afternoon. But the flow seemed blocked; the connections, forced.

During the next few years, we worked through the issues of time and access. We now schedule the full day in an oversized room where computers sit in clusters along the periphery and seminar tables in the middle can accommodate the whole class. At any time of day, we can now move freely from discussion or journal writing to developing a paper on the computer. Better access and more flexibility have made the course "feel" like a writing project again.

In an ideal setting, all writers have regular access to pens, pencils, paper, printouts, word processing software, file disks, and computers. And they have access to computers often enough to become fluent on them.

Time is available for the whole writing process. Students may do prewriting by hand or by machine, but they have several sessions at the computer to draft and revise on the basis of feedback. A writer may return to a draft days or weeks after it was "finished," call up the file, and revise again.

Most of us still don't work in an ideal setting. During the five years I've watched teachers using new writing tools, schools have greatly increased their stock of computers. But at the same time, more writing teachers have become computer literate, a growing clientele of users that competes for a growing supply of tools. The result in most schools is that each student's real access time has increased very little.

Our teachers have found the following suggestions helpful when trying to build a WritingLand with minimal access time:

1. *Do short, collaborative, much-revised pieces like the ones suggested for getting started (see chapter 6).* Tackling a major research paper with minimal access will cause your writers more frustration than it's worth.

2. *Concentrate access so that writers get to the computers several times, a day or two apart.* Better one good "immersion" experience than a series of brief visits to the lab. Students need time to feel at home in a WritingLand.

3. *Negotiate for substantial blocks of class time; avoid the half-hour period.* At the beginning and end of a lab session, you'll need extra minutes for booting up, getting files, saving, and printing. Be sure there's enough time in the middle for writing activity.

4. *Synchronize classroom activities with lab activities.* Planning and peer response don't require computer access; drafting and revision and publishing final copy do.

5. *Try to be with your writers while they compose at the computers. If that's impossible, team-plan with your lab teacher.* But remember Becky's experience: there's really no substitute for being there.

12 Space, Layout, and Supervision

Writers need space to spread out drafts, notes, and reference books. They need flexible layouts where peer partners can collaborate, groups can meet, and teachers can walk around for conferences. They also need flexible rules that support their attempts to manage their own writing processes. In most schools, students don't work in settings that meet these needs.

Frank Smith (1982) comments that "professional writers would perhaps be unable to write at all in the constrained and inhibiting circumstances in which children are often expected to write at school" (206). In most classrooms, students have neither the privacy to ponder nor the freedom to talk. They can't indulge their own comfortable writing rituals. (I like to write with opera music, black coffee, and chocolate pie; my son, Adam Pablo, drafts in his bed with rap music and a bag of tortilla chips.) In a classroom, when writers are suffering writer's block, they can't ball up papers and toss them from their desks. They can't stomp and yell to let off steam. They can rarely even get up and walk around or ask a friend for help.

A computer lab that was not designed for writing tends to be less supportive still. Students and teachers cope with cramped working space and rigid layout, as well as the time constraints discussed in chapter 11. Math and business labs seem designed to cram the largest number of computers into the smallest number of square feet. Machines are set close together in straight rows, and often the workstations are bolted to the floor for security. Try writing in this kind of environment!

I've learned that the physical setting of the computers has a great impact on their value to a writing program. Our teachers have identified four settings which can be appropriate to a WritingLand. We can place computers:

1. *as audio-visual equipment in a traditional classroom;*

2. *as a writing center in an open classroom;*

3. *as a support in a tutorial writing facility;*

4. *as the focus of activity in a variety of computer labs.*

110

Traditional Classroom

Writing classes can benefit from word processing even without access to a lab. Our teachers have brought a single computer on a rolling cart into classes ranging from seven to twenty-five writers. They found many successful applications.

Pairs of students may take turns doing introductory activities on one computer, usually in preparation for a longer activity in a lab. For example, the teacher may call one student to the workstation and demonstrate how to call up a file and type a greeting ("Hi! This is Jane signing on!"). Each student in turn guides the next writer through the task. At the end, the teacher prints out and posts the roster.

An extensive class project may be based on just one mobile unit. Joann Hynes's small group of basic writers (see chapter 6) used a single computer to gather their research on teenage problems and to publish their book of community resources.

Most often, the computer hooked up with special cables to a large television monitor or an overhead projector becomes a prized piece of audiovisual equipment. You can use this arrangement to model the writing process in action. Simply type passages from student papers, sentence-combining problems, or literary selections on a disk and then call up the file for student response.

Anne Wright frequently rolls a single computer and large monitor into her senior composition classes. She chooses one student's essay to display and has the whole class work together as a peer group. The teacher guides and models helpful response. The writer maintains "author-ity" over the keyboard and over the revision process.

We videotaped on the day the class critiqued Paul's lead paragraph to his essay on Browning's "My Last Duchess." Paul sat at the computer in front of the room, listening as peers discussed his work, asked questions, and gave suggestions. When Paul accepted the feedback, he keyed in a revision. The videotape shows unusual concentration on the faces of these students as they watched the passage glowing on the screen and considered each revision Paul typed.

At the University of Missouri–St. Louis, the English department keeps the same type of monitor on a rolling cart in the computer workroom. When instructors want to do a demonstration, they set the laptop computer on the cart, plug the cables into the monitor, and roll the equipment down the hall, onto the elevator, and into their writing class.

If you have control over your own classroom space and minimal access to computers, your students will probably gain more from frequent demonstrations on the rolling cart than from infrequent visits to the lab.

Open Classroom with Learning Center

One or more computers are sometimes placed, not on a cart, but directly in a writing classroom. For Peggy Ryan (see chapter 2), two workstations fit naturally into the environment of an open classroom with learning centers. Such an arrangement best suits teachers who are already accustomed to working with groups, guiding writers through the process at their own pace, and individualizing assignments, deadlines, and standards. For them, the in-class word-processing center is ideal.

To schedule lab access, a teacher must plan lessons so that every writer is ready to enter text at the same time. How can you know in March that a paper will be ready to draft or revise on the second Tuesday in April? But when the computers are housed permanently in the classroom, writers can gravitate toward them at any point in their own process.

You might begin with a whole-class prewriting session and then send the students one at a time to the computers to develop their text. When everyone's turn ends, after twenty or thirty minutes, each of them prints a double-spaced draft and lets the new writers take their places at the keyboard. The next day, the students get feedback from peers, and then they revise at the computer.

You could follow the same sequence in a lab if you have frequent access, but the difference is in flexibility. Students in an open setting move freely from word processing to other tasks and back again. If they notice an error on a "final" printout, they can usually get access for a few minutes, edit, and reprint.

Placing one or two computers permanently in a classroom is not cost-effective in a teacher-directed program that stresses lecture and whole-class instruction. There, the computer would often remain idle, perhaps being restricted to the last minutes of class. But in a student-centered program, the computer makes a fine classroom writing center.

Tutorial Writing Center

In most schools today, computers are placed in labs. The term "lab," however, is used for several quite-different settings, including tutorial centers and larger staffed or unstaffed facilities. I'll discuss each of these settings in turn. The small, drop-in tutorial lab can be a resource for the entire school. The center is staffed by a writing specialist, perhaps one teacher all day, perhaps several on a part-time basis. The specialist may be assisted by trained peer tutors. Students work at the computer in the presence of people who know how to help with writing problems and can provide brief process conferences.

Such centers have long been common at the college level. Recently, they have spread to the junior and senior high schools, sometimes sparked by the arrival of computers, sometimes planned simply as conference rooms without any electronic support. Pamela Farrell's new book, *The High School Writing Center: Establishing and Maintaining One* (1989), is a much-needed resource and includes several chapters by our St. Louis teachers.

A tutorial lab can help with remedial tutoring, college applications, content-area papers, writing contests, and publications. Typically, a center houses just a few computers, which may be supplemented by those in a nearby computer lab.

At suburban Webster Groves High School, teachers wrote a state grant requesting six computers and one faculty member's released time to develop a tutorial lab. They share the faculty position so that each teacher staffs the facility one period of the day. Students can request a pass to the lab just as they would a pass to the school library. At the lab, they can find individual help for specific writing needs.

One drawback is that the lab's specialist is rarely the student's own English teacher. Since that teacher must stay with the whole class, integration between work in the tutorial lab and in the English course may be minimal. Webster Groves solves this problem by sending students to the lab with a referral sheet that explains the assignment, the purpose of the tutoring, or the nature of the project.

Computer Lab

When visiting schools, I was startled at the contrasts I found between two kinds of labs that seem to differ merely in size. Both are general-purpose labs serving all subject areas. Unlike the tutorial writing centers, they are not staffed by writing teachers. But large labs and small or medium labs tend to offer quite different environments for writers.

The most common setting for computers is a medium-sized lab created from an extra classroom, study center, or library alcove. Typically, the lab holds about a dozen computers arranged in rows.

Writing teachers send half a class to the lab on a rotating basis, where they are usually supervised by an aide or a parent volunteer. The teacher may do a mini-lesson in class, with enough prewriting to prepare most students to draft or revise at the computer. Once there, writers are on their own. The lab supervisor, seldom trained in process approaches to writing, helps mainly with such technical matters as supplies, commands, and filenames.

This is the least supportive environment for writers. They have no access to a writing teacher while they are actually writing with the computers. It was in this kind of lab that Becky had to abandon her lion. Her writing teacher would have responded to a time crunch in a way that honored her story, but the computer teacher focused on technical skills.

Just when I'd given up on all-purpose computer labs, I noticed certain schools where they were serving writers very well. The successful labs were much larger, though equipped with the same dozen or so computers. Simply increasing the size of the room seemed to improve the learning conditions dramatically. I wondered why.

A large lab has space for a whole class to move around in. Computers don't need to be jammed together. They can be stationed along the periphery while the middle of the room holds enough desks or tables to allow a typical class to spread out and write. These labs may be staffed by an aide, a computer teacher, a writing specialist, a parent—or nobody at all. But their size makes it easy for a writing teacher to accompany a whole class instead of sending some students to work on their own.

At Lindbergh High School's lab, John Weiss usually starts class with everybody grouped in the middle at desks for a mini-lesson or a review of procedures. Then half the students move to the computers while the other half work at the desks, writing individually or meeting with peers. Their regular writing teacher is available to all of them throughout the process. He gives brief, over-the-shoulder conferences to those at the computers or answers editorial questions from the peer groups. A lab supervisor, if present, could add extra technical help.

Eventually, after seeing many labs, I realized that the issue was not size but support. How well a lab works depends on the quality of support writers can get while they are actually engaged in writing. If gaining access to a new writing tool means that students will lose access to a skilled writing teacher, the trade-off is simply not worth it.

Designing Space and Layout

If your school's only lab has a dozen computers jammed in rows, don't despair. Perhaps the writing staff can sponsor a free lunch for the math department in the hope of gaining some allies for a new design. Perhaps an administrator will agree to make some changes in the lab.

After observing computer environments for several years, I found the Gateway Writing Project's summer institute scheduled in just such an all-purpose lab. (It even looked depressing, stuck in a windowless basement.) After grumbling into various deaf ears, we decided to move the seventeen computers down the hall to a large media center which was lightly scheduled during summer school.

Long tables used for laminating and slide preparation each served very nicely for two computers plus a workspace. Smaller round tables invited peer groups. A giant television monitor was available, so we hooked up a single computer for demonstrations. For part of the day we had to share this space with students who were making audiovisual materials, so we scheduled our own peer group meetings to run concurrently. The ambience was a bit hectic, but it worked.

Two years ago, we found a different solution. Going back to the original basement lab, we rearranged the equipment. We broke up the rows, placing the computers along the periphery. Instead of facing outward, which would isolate writers and make it hard to see demonstrations, the workstations were set in pairs that jutted out from the walls. Writers could simply pivot their chairs to face forward. We left the teacher's desk in front, adding the computer and big television screen on a rolling cart. Then we asked the janitors for some long tables, the folding kind that are kept in storage for special events like graduation. We set these in rows down the now-vacant middle.

Our makeshift lab is so crowded that we need a break-out room to leave briefcases, lunches, or umbrellas. (Peer groups meet in the cafeteria over coffee.) But we can teach in this place, and we can write and talk and conference. When it feels claustrophobic, we remind ourselves that a WritingLand is a social environment!

Even a small, unstaffed computer lab, normally the least supportive setting, can be salvaged for writers. Pattonville High School acquired an all-purpose lab, a dozen computers in straight rows in a spare classroom. Due to a shortage of rooms, the lab had to share space with a tiny writing center. The result was a teacherless lab that flowed into a tutoring and conferencing facility: a WritingLand suite. Here a teacher can send half a class to the lab knowing that students will have access to the writing teacher who staffs the center.

Lillian Atchison's small lab, which is adjacent to the library, works in much the same way. The writing teacher can accompany a whole class while half of the students use the computers and the other half do research in the library. In both of these situations, the small, unstaffed lab is contiguous with a place where students *can* get help during the process of writing.

Designing a computer-equipped place that supports writers does not need to cost more than designing a place that hampers them. But it requires the leadership and vision of people who understand how a writing community works.

13 Hardware and Software

When It All Goes Wrong

Marilyn Dell'Orco was regretting that she'd ever seen a computer. Her school had a network of seven terminals, only one of them a "master" unit with disk drives and a printer. This equipment worked very well for the math teacher, who had recruited parent volunteers to staff the tiny lab and liked to send a half-dozen students to practice long division and least common denominators with gamelike software.

At times Dell'Orco had also used the lab for grammar games, but now she wanted to teach real writing. After a summer with the Gateway Writing Project, she'd acquired an "easy" word-processing package for her brand of computers and looked forward to helping her seventh and eighth graders write and publish.

Then her troubles began. Students loved writing by machine, and they loved getting printouts. But they couldn't make the computers save to a disk. Every visit to the lab meant retyping their whole text. The students didn't complain because they were used to recopying any time they revised by hand. In fact, since they could get access to the lab only once every couple of weeks, they often drafted a text on the computer, and then revised and rewrote a final copy with pen and paper! They were missing the point of what word processing could do for them.

For six months Dell'Orco fought with a network that wouldn't communicate and disk drives that wouldn't save. She spent hours on the phone with the store that handled her equipment. She watched a parade of their "expert consultants" arrive at the lab, each cheerfully predicting that the problem was minor. They would fuss with the machines for an hour, call a supervisor for advice, and then leave, promising to return soon with the solution.

The most baffling part of her network was its unpredictability. Although it never saved, sometimes it would print, and other times it ignored all commands and reverted to BASIC. Losing faith in her expert consultants, she sought divine intervention:

> My seventh graders worked diligently in the computer lab. Before

117

> printing their work, I read it and was impressed. . . . I prayed to
> the god of computers and the god of printers, and miraculously
> I received a printout.

But a month later, her troubles returned:

> I checked all connections, pressed different keys, gave new com-
> mands, and inserted new paper, but the printer was stubborn. I
> ranted, raved, kicked, and called Expert Consultant No. 4. All
> this was to no avail. Two computers locked up and three reverted
> to BASIC; it was a 29 percent day.

Finally, in March, a month before we were scheduled to present together at a national conference, I phoned the company's headquarters to suggest that our presentation might be embarrassing to them.

The next week, Expert Consultant No. 5 found the problem: the wrong version of DOS. A teacher and her students—and their files— were saved. Her conference paper (from which I've been quoting) bore the wry-yet-optimistic title: "God, What Hath DOS Wrought?" (Dell'Orco 1985). It's an instructive case history of what can happen with computers in the wrong learning environment: a small lab where students work from time to time (chapter 11) without any support for the writing process (chapter 12).

Still, more dramatically, Dell'Orco's tale shows how the wrong hardware and software can sabotage plans for a WritingLand. Her system had been marketed by an electronics firm at prices below the major brands and with service to match. It wasn't designed or purchased with writing in mind. Networking seven terminals with just one pair of disk drives and one printer would bring the most computer for the least money—and math games don't need to be saved or printed. But that equipment would never support a community of writers. At the end of every class, the parent aide faced a crisis with seven writers demanding hard copy from one printer. (Once they turned off their networked machines, the unsaved text was gone forever.)

The word-processing software was also wrong. It was "command driven" rather than "menu driven": students memorize the commands to delete, insert, move, etc., or else consult a manual. (That's fine if writers have enough access to memorize the commands naturally or enough skilled tutors to get help from quickly. But a minimally supervised lab calls for the easiest software; menus defining all commands visible right on screen.)

A more subtle problem is that the wrong equipment makes the computer the center of attention, when it should be a tool that supports writing and learning. During those frustrating months, students enjoyed going to the lab because it was a novelty, a chance to play on the computers. They couldn't use the system to develop significant papers, with peer response and revision. But they could have fun for an hour updating a Christmas carol in teenage slang, and they could join their teacher in prayer for a printout. Going to the lab was an experiment in word processing, not an experience in writing.

Learning to Make the Tools Invisible

Marilyn Dell'Orco's story sounds like an extreme case; after that initiation, I admired her good humor in continuing with the action research. But most of us have at least one horror story about the day we were upstaged by a computer. When we begin teaching in a lab, we just can't handle the equipment smoothly.

The first summer that Gateway used computers, I often faced twenty-five tolerantly smiling teachers as I fought with cables, adapters, and software—sometimes at last to succeed, sometimes finally to cancel my well-planned presentation. I felt like an idiot. And the computer certainly did not seem like a wonderful tool that was helping me build a community of writers. That computer was an uncooperative piece of newfangled audiovisual equipment that was stealing the limelight from whatever I was trying to teach and from whatever my class was trying to write.

Only after some experience did I find computers retreating from center stage and agreeing to become a supporting cast of writing tools. Today, after five years, the technology is almost transparent in Gateway Writing Project workshops. We teach most computer skills inductively, in the context of a process approach to writing. Today, I can lead an inservice for teachers with no computer experience and still keep the focus on composing. That didn't happen at first, though, regardless of my enthusiasm for computers as tools. Be patient with yourself as you learn *not* to let the tools steal the show from the writing.

A Rhetoric of Writing Tools

I've been saying that hardware and software should be unobtrusive in a WritingLand. On the other hand, sometimes it's useful to make tools the focus of a lesson—deliberately.

We ask students to reflect on how the computer shapes their own composing processes (Madigan 1984). Do you edit more willingly? Do you miss seeing the whole paper when the screen shows only twenty-four lines? We compare the computer with the more traditional writing tools, asking which works best for a specific purpose and audience (Flinn 1987b). Try these questions to help writers view technology realistically—so that they'll know when a computer will be an asset and when it may be a frill.

If we write the names of several alternative tools on the board, high school students may generate ideas such as those in the following paragraphs.

Chalk. Writing is slow, often awkward. As we move the chalk faster, the writing gets harder to read; we trade fluency in writing for fluency in reading. The text is easy to delete and replace with a board eraser, but there is no way to do a block move without recopying. Since chalkboards are not portable, this tool is limited to classroom writing.

Pencil. Writing speed is average. We again have a trade-off between writing and reading fluency. The text is easy to change, since the writer can delete and change with an eraser or move blocks with scissors and tape. The tool is cheap and portable, so writing can happen anywhere.

Pen. Like the pencil, a pen gives an average writing speed and a trade-off between writing and reading. The text is usually more legible than in pencil because it contrasts vividly with the paper. But it is not easy to change; although text-block movements can be made by cutting and taping, the text can't often be erased, and scratching out makes it hard to read. The tool is portable and usually cheap.

Typewriter. Writing can be fast—for a touch typist. It's slow for students using the hunt-and-peck method. Text is very legible, with no trade-off between writing and reading speed, except for added typos. But text is awkward to change: arrows and crossing out make it hard to read, while whiteout and correction tape make it hard to write. Moving blocks of text means pulling the whole paper from the machine to cut and tape. And "portable" doesn't mean that you can take this tool along on a field trip.

Computer. Writing can be fast—for a touch typist who knows the software. For most students, first drafting is slow, but the time saved in recopying more than compensates. Text is legible (limited by the twenty-four-line screen and resolution) at any writing speed. It is also very flexible, allowing the writer to delete, replace, add, or move text without recopying. But the tool is not portable; even students with home computers can rarely use a disk prepared at school.

Reflecting on their own tools puts writers, not computers, in charge of the process. If rhetoric is the art of making wise linguistic choices, perhaps students should also learn a rhetoric of writing tools: how to choose the right tool for a particular purpose, audience, and process of writing.

While watching students experiment with writing tools, I've noticed an odd pattern. A combination of tools (hand drafting, word processing, jotting on printout) seems to be an asset. Once text is typed on disk, it is easy to call up and change, so I assumed students would do most of their revision after typing. In fact, they did the opposite. Writers made more changes and tackled revisions of larger units at the point when they first translated handwritten text onto the computer (Daiute 1985 confirms the same observation). Once typed, the text received mainly surface editing at the computer.

I don't understand this. We've all seen students merely recopy literally from draft to draft; however, when they recopy onto the computer they tend to make changes as they go along. Perhaps the very act of transcribing in a different medium jogs them free from the tyranny of their own first drafts. Writers of all ages seem to revise more thoroughly when they use more than one writing tool per paper.

When thinking about writing tools, we need to remember that looking at a screen is quite different from looking at a page. Cindy Selfe (1989) points to the conventions: the printed page is a structural unit of a longer text which a reader can flip through and perceive spatially; screens are "temporal windows on a virtual text" which can be seen as a whole only in a reader's mind (7). The formats also differ: a screen is flexible, with margins that change and a shape more like a television than a book. Since most writers become literate on paper first, they must add another "layer" of literacy when using the computer. To teach this "layered literacy," we must deal with new conventions; writers may show emphasis on screen through highlighting, color, and special fonts as well as through punctuation (7–13).

Selfe offers a model that all writing teachers can use. As the technology of writing continues to grow, we need to focus on our core issues of rhetoric and literacy. We—and our students—need to talk about the experience as we try new writing tools and make them our own.

Tools for a WritingLand

Throughout this book, the tools I've described have generally been low-tech. They are the tools Gateway Writing Project teachers have actually used with their classes, the tools our action research has been able to assess in context. I can observe the cutting edge of technology at a conference, but I see much simpler tools when observing in classrooms.

What tools should you buy with a typically limited school budget? I can't promote specific brands of computers or specific software packages. (I won't even pan the corporation of expert consultants.) When the technology changes so quickly, a few guidelines will prove more useful.

Hardware

In a WritingLand, the basic hardware should be as ample as funds allow. Each *computer* used for writing needs at least one disk drive; more powerful word-processing programs and integrated software packages will usually require two disk drives. Each computer also needs easy access to a *printer*. An *A-B switch* can link two computers to one printer; otherwise you must either switch the cables or switch disks, files, and students. (The A-B switch will spare your nerves.) One printer for two or three computers is an efficient ratio for a lab serving writers who face deadlines and tardy bells.

Whole-class teaching with computers requires a few additional items. Start with a *projection device* to roll into class or demonstrate in the lab. I've described lessons where a computer is hooked to a large television monitor; newer equipment based on the overhead projector is more legible and more portable. After the computers and printers, a projection device is likely to be your most valued piece of hardware. Add a slick, *white marking board*, since chalk dust can harm computers.

One less-common piece of hardware with great potential for schools is the *modem*. Students can join with students in the same city or around the world (Levin et al. 1985; Spitzer 1989). They can produce a joint newspaper, write up the results of collaborative research, send letters via electronic mail, or exchange news on a bulletin board. The modem and software are not expensive, but they require a separate phone line. This bit of old technology has posed enough of a problem that teachers in our project have not made much use of teleconferencing. But I'm convinced that a modem can bring exciting new audiences to a WritingLand.

Labs in the St. Louis public schools have computers linked in a *network* to a viewing station on the teacher's desk. This equipment can help or inhibit the writing process, depending on how it's used. Process-oriented teachers find it supports peer response. They send Tom's file to Larry's screen, and then Larry types his feedback and sends the whole file back to Tom. But I've also seen teachers misuse the link to avoid conferencing. For example, they may check on a writer's progress by calling the file up to their own screen and perhaps typing some comments. Much better to walk around the lab, pat a shoulder, and talk about the writing as an interested reader.

Software

For teaching writing, software begins with the essential, all-purpose tool, *word processing*. Put the bulk of a software budget into a first-rate package to be used throughout a building. The basic software does word processing alone. Newer, integrated packages do word processing, spelling, databases, and, perhaps, tutorials with the same kinds of commands and the same disks. The best word processing programs for writing classes will have easy-to-remember commands ("Control-S" rather than "Control-K-D" for "Save") and optional menus to help new users learn them.

The word processor is fundamentally different from most educational software. I discovered this when I took a course in BASIC for teachers. Our assignment was to write an interactive program for a lesson we ordinarily taught with conventional materials. For a writing teacher, the task was harder than it appeared.

I decided to adapt a sentence expansion activity which had been successful with my basic writers. I'd present a list of kernel sentences consisting of a subject-verb core:

> The dog barks.
> The President speaks.
> The lovers whisper.

Students would find the subjects and verbs, and then expand with the most outrageous modifiers at hand to produce such masterpieces as "The mangy brown and white dog in the yard next door barks frantically all night long at the tabby cat on the back fence." Later, students would create their own kernels, pass them to a classmate to expand, and then pass them to another classmate to find the original kernels. We often applied the concept of sentence expansion when talking about professional or student writing: no matter how complicated the style, you could always contract the main clause to a subject-verb core. Variations of this lesson had worked well on a purple ditto, on an overhead, and on a chalkboard.

So I set to work at the computer, programming my lesson in BASIC. I imagined the program as a sort of script: the computer says a few lines; then the student has space to reply. "Expand 'dog' with a prepositional phrase, Sarah" prompts the computer. If Sarah types "in the yard," the program deftly plugs in the modifier and displays "dog in the yard." But some English modifiers can go either before or after a noun ("the old, mangy dog" or "the dog, old and mangy"), a quirk the computer language can't handle. I tried to anticipate all sorts of options in every kernel sentence, entering each laboriously into my program.

Finally, after more than a thousand lines of BASIC and more than a hundred hours of labor, I had an interactive program covering about half the material on my original one-page ditto! Unlike my ditto, this program could be used only in a specific setting (a Commodore lab) and in a specific sequence (start to finish, give or take a few feedback loops in response to errors). When I wanted students to compose their own kernel sentences, I had to program instructions that sent them beyond the computer: "Now, Sarah, take your journal and write. . . ."

I got an A on that programming assignment, but I've never used the software with a single class. Instead, it showed me that word processing is the key technology for writers because it supports natural language. Today, to adapt a good writing lesson for the computer, I simply type it on a file disk with the software my students normally use for writing.

My sentence expansion lesson takes about fifteen minutes to type, and it works beautifully with the word processor. Students call up the file, read my typed instructions (no programmed prompts, thank you, just plain English), and move the cursor to insert their modifiers. BASIC can't predict English word order, but basic writers can. They intuitively know where an adjective sounds right, and they like to experiment by moving words around.

So after one try at programming, and many more at reviewing commercial interactive software, I suggest word processing as the main tool for a WritingLand. While you can buy separate programs for prewriting or sentence combining, writers can usually do just as well with lesson files typed on your word processor. Good samples are available in books by Rodrigues and Rodrigues (1986) and Franklin and Madian (1988). Some word-processing programs designed for schools can produce "frozen text," the teacher's questions and prompts which remain unchanged as students enter and revise their own writing. The frozen text is omitted when students print out a document, which saves paper.

The next priority should be software that interfaces with the word processor and supports some phase of the writing process. A *spelling checker* and *homonym checker* are real assets; be sure they are authorable, so that you can add your own special items to the lists. A simple spelling checker flags any word that doesn't match its dictionary (this will include proper names), and then asks the writer whether to correct it or leave it alone.

Newer spelling checkers also offer a list of possible correct spellings, usually any nearby word or anagram in the dictionary. Our teachers have mixed feelings about this enhancement. Some find that the list helps really weak spellers, who then check their best guess in a conventional dictionary. Others find that students pick their best guess and check no further, sometimes choosing electronic malapropisms. Recently Nancy Cason's seventh graders tried proofreading for the first time with one of the enhanced spelling checkers. Words were flagged by the software and students could *choose* one of the suggested spellings, *ignore* the warning, or *type* in their own correction. Table 5 shows how they responded.

The seventh graders were enthusiastic about this proofreading session. "I like these spell-checks," grinned one writer. But a review of the feedback they received left us doubtful. The list of on-screen choices often omitted the correct spelling, even of such common errors as "alot." With the simpler type of spelling checker, kids sit at the computer with a dictionary on their laps, checking the words as they're marked. With the list of suggestions, it is tempting to guess. Perhaps Cason's students were simply responding to this feedback as inexperienced users. We have observed that writers do learn in time to double-check the spelling checker—usually by asking a peer or an adult for help with an unlikely set of choices. Perhaps teachers can guide a whole class through a few items to show that software, too, makes mistakes and that the author must have author-ity over the tool.

Like spelling and homonym checkers, other search-and-find programs can flag anything from boring words to sexist titles. Late Secretary of Commerce Malcolm Baldrige programmed his department's word processors to flag such bureaucratic terms as "viable" and "utilize." Now that's progress!

Some of the *prewriting and revision programs* are worth buying, especially those which are integrated with your word processor for easy access. An interactive program may ask writers to state topic, audience, and purpose as they plan their texts. Valarie Arms (1988) reports that her engineering students enjoyed nonverbal planning with MACPAINT; first they predrew a design and then explained it in words. More powerful computers with hypercard technology can give students access to whole libraries of information and to the direct experience of art and music as they plan. An outliner, guiding writers both to plan and to check their organization, is well suited to long pieces of writing like the research paper. Some revision programs will pull out one sentence at a time to call students' attention to potential run-ons or to report information on readability, sentence length, and target structures.

Yet, even programs geared to the writing process may subvert it. Lisa Gerrard (1989) warns, "As passive learners, many basic writers accept feedback they don't understand, rather than questioning and learning from it" (102). (If some of our eighth graders wouldn't argue with a spelling checker, what would they do with a usage program?) The editing and style analysis programs our teachers have reviewed are notoriously unreliable. Try any such programs yourself with text you actually write. See if the response fits what you would say to your students.

Freestanding programs—tutorials on essay organization, or gamelike programs on grammatical structures—have limited use. Check to see if they provide for any transfer to actual student writing. (Some of the better ones contain a basic word processor or require students to compose a piece demonstrating that they can use the target structure correctly.) Unfortunately, most of these programs are modeled on workbook exercises. Kids may have more fun blasting adverbs than underlining them, but the application to writing is just as limited.

While a WritingLand may function well without most of the commercial programs, save a generous chunk of your software budget for *graphics and desktop publishing*. Writers take pride in illustrating a story or designing a report cover with the help of the computer. The simplest programs will print a set of drawings in various sizes, from note cards to banners. Graphics programs which are linked to word processors will produce columns of text for newsletters or fancy fonts for artistic printing.

Our notion of rhetoric might be expanded to include such visual communication. Art teacher Beverly Phillips asks young writers to review their partners' drafts and the graphics chosen to illustrate them. Peer groups ask how well the graphics fit the text and support its message. Bev Hopkins uses three questions for peer response to illustrations (Melton 1985):

> Will the illustration encourage the reader to read the text?
> Can it be seen six feet away?
> How can it be improved?

The *database* is a wonderful tool for building research skills. Indi-

Table 5
How Seventh Graders Applied Feedback on Spelling[1]

Student's Spelling	Feedback: Software	Feedback: Human	Student's Response
missles	missiles	—	*Chose* correct item.
poped	pooped, piped, etc.	adult	Looked puzzled; guessed "popped." Checked with adult; *typed* correctly.
shure	shire, shore, sure, etc. (mid list)	peer: "there's no *h* in it!"	Did not see correct item; rejected peer advice. *Ignored.*
dissaper	dissenter, diaper, etc.	—	Hit *ignore;* did not try to correct.
disapered	disappeared	—	*Chose* correct item.
youngens	younger, youngest	adult: "That's oral, good in story but not in dictionary."	Discussed with adult the best spelling for dialect term. *Typed* "young'uns."
alot	allot, alto, aloha, etc.	adult	Scanned list; asked adult, That's right, isn't it?" "No, it's 2 words." *Typed* "a lot."
scape	scale, scrape, etc.	adult	*Typed* "asape." Adult coached, "read slowly out loud." *Typed* "escape."
Capitan	capital, capitol, captain (end of list)	peer	Began to *type* correction; then peer spotted it. *Chose* correct item.
Capitan	same	—	Third occurrence; promptly *chose* correct item from end of list.

vidual writers can store and alphabetize information for a research paper, or a group can collaborate in gathering data for a class project. If the database is flexible, try a lesson in which students draw on the same information for different purposes, with different principles of organization.

Norma Owen uses a "gifted persons database" with such items as dates of birth and death, major achievements, failures, parents' occupations, birth order, and amount of formal education. Her advanced sixth graders sort the data on different fields (for example, by position in family) and then write their conclusions: Does birth order make a difference? Is the percentage of firstborns in our class similar to that in the database of gifted persons? How do you feel about your own position in your family and its impact on you? Databases lend themselves to many kinds of writing. Social studies teacher Michael Pfefferkorn has designed a set of fields to help his eleventh graders record data for their genealogy projects. Several of our elementary teachers use a class database of book reviews, which can be printed out and posted in the classroom.

Finally, consider *utilities* such as communications software (for the modem), a subscription to an online encyclopedia, and a simple program for storing grades and other class records.

When you plan the equipment for a WritingLand, keep it simple. Begin with just a few items. Once you have them integrated into your own way of teaching writing, you can add more powerful hardware, more innovative software.

But whatever you buy, keep the focus on writing. Evaluate new programs by how well they support a process approach to teaching writing. You may or may not be on the cutting edge of technology. But the microcomputer used for word processing will probably remain the essential tool for writers.

Notes

1. Feedback from a spelling checker integrated with the Bank Street Writer III (New York: Scholastic 1986).

14 Teachers

The main character in any WritingLand is the teacher. This is especially true in learner-centered workshops such as those described by Donald Murray (1985) or Nancie Atwell (1987), which may *seem* to minimize direct teaching. I've said earlier that we create a sort of counterpoint: we design classroom experiences of prewriting, drafting, and editing with feedback which we believe will guide students through the recursive processes of composing. The teacher's art comes in responding to writers in a way that supports rather than disrupts their process.

Sarah Freedman's (1987) study shows that teachers who play leading roles in the National Writing Project do this quite differently from teachers in general. She found that NWP teachers assigned writing more often, both in and outside of class, with longer pieces being developed over a period of time. They responded often to writing in progress, aiming at problem solving and critical awareness. Finally, they valued writing for multiple purposes—not information *or* expression, not content *or* skills, but all of them in context. Our teachers in St. Louis are working in this NWP tradition of response to the process.

The computer inevitably changes how we provide this support. Teaching well with new writing tools prompts us to make subtle but significant changes in how we manage a writing workshop. Teachers discover new approaches to conferencing, to publishing and other projects, and to curriculum development. They learn along with their students, so together they find new patterns of leadership.

Individual Conferences

"I don't comment much on final copy," explains John Weiss, "because it's dead. My feedback comes in floating around the lab as students work on drafts." Here is a glimpse of conferencing in his twelfth-grade advanced composition class.

Brett sits at the keyboard mulling over a description of his Dad reading the newspaper in a red flannel housecoat. His teacher suggests eliminating a wordy lead: "Get yourself out of the picture—delete that junk and then fiddle with it. Pretend you're a movie director—*show* Dad!"

I watch this teacher make the rounds of the lab, pausing often to scan a monitor and offer some feedback. This time he reads Brett's new opening line with admiration; then he asks him to find another sentence that needs work. Brett points to an interminable line describing the housecoat. "Bisect it someplace!" urges his teacher with mock horror. Brett thinks of a possible revision, but hesitates: "Well, try it out! Is anybody going to slice your fingers off? If you don't like it, you can always change it on the computer." The tough coaching is brightened by laughter and affirmation.

A process approach to writing emphasizes the one-to-one conference while students are drafting. But elementary and secondary teachers struggle with heavy schedules and lack of conference time. Gail Taylor explains how she marshalled the many resources of a WritingLand to individualize proofreading instruction for a seventh-grade basic writer:

> After Alex had his paper fairly well typed, I talked to him about the run-on sentences. I did this by writing on his paper, "Please read this out loud so you can tell where to put the periods." He understood why this worked because I had, on several occasions, read his paper aloud for him. He was able to listen to his actual words that way, instead of what he thought he had on paper. [Alex then read aloud to another student and inserted some periods.]
>
> Our next task was spelling. Alex used the spell checker, and with the aid of the dictionary and those around him, managed to spell almost all of the words correctly. . . .
>
> The final thing we worked on was paragraphing [since his whole paper] had one long paragraph. I began reading the paper aloud, and he would say, "Oh, a new paragraph should start there." The rest of the paper he marked on his own. Then he went back to the computer, put the cursor where the paragraph should be, hit Return, and spaced over to indent.

Notice that, instead of one long conference, this teacher relies on several brief meetings, each focused on one problem at a time. Here the computer is our ally. Because the student's text is public, legible on a screen and ready to modify, a new opportunity for conferencing is created.

These brief conferences tend to be more productive than many traditional ones. Susan Florio-Ruane's research (1986) finds most writing conferences dominated by teachers: too often, the writer simply "hands over" a text for comments. Similarly, a study by Sally Fitzgerald (1988) finds teachers using conference time mainly to point out errors.

Watching our own teachers doing brief conferences at the computer,

I found a different pattern. The writer retains control, "hands on" the keyboard, as the teacher bends over to watch, suggest, but rarely to change the text. Some teachers deliberately alter the physical setting to keep the writer in control. Theresa Simon explains,

> This year I used a small stool to sit next to groups and individuals so that I was near and on their level. During two-minute conferences over grades, my [ninth graders] sat on a taller stool while I was in my desk chair.

In a WritingLand, even beginning authors can claim their own authority as they get feedback from a teacher who assumes the role of interested reader.

Group Conferences

Most of our teachers conference with groups of writers as well as with individuals. These meetings give them an occasion to check on the feedback peers are sharing and to model constructive response.

Watch as Joan Thomas meets with one peer group at a round table in the corner of their eighth-grade classroom. Today Ingrid holds her draft, a printout with penned-in revisions, and begins by telling her audience and purpose.

"I'm writing to parents," she says, "to inform them how to set reasonable expectations for their children." Then she lists specific areas where she wants help: "What I'm concerned about is repetition of words. It seems like in every sentence I have 'expectations' or 'situation' or something like that. Also I'm not sure if I have enough facts or details."

As Ingrid reads aloud, her group and her teacher listen, taking notes. Andy draws a line down his page, jotting what he likes on one side, what he doesn't like on the other: "I like the way you gave suggestions, what they should do and what they shouldn't do. You know, don't do this because it would lower your kids' self-esteem."

John adds, "You don't just say to the parents, 'Do this!' You say, 'If you do this, that may happen.' "

Their teacher decides to elaborate: "I liked the tone, too. It's not preachy, but you give practical advice. During the intro I could see parents nodding their heads."

At this point the group responds to Ingrid's two concerns, which turn out to be connected. The paper sometimes gets stuck at a very general and abstract level, without the examples that would make the abstractions real. Her listeners point out problem areas, recite the sentences aloud, and try to explain what they think Ingrid means. She, of course, gets into the discussion, struggling to make her meaning clear. According to her draft, "When parents have too high expectations, even perfection becomes more than perfection." The group helps her translate, "When parents expect perfection, even an A seems like an A− because it's not an A+."

Ingrid and her peers are competent eighth graders, but group conferencing can be just as helpful to students with a history of failure. After two years of action research with underachieving black writers, Joan Krater Thomas has refined her approach to build confidence and skill. She guides her basic students through each phase of the process, with modeling, personal support, and collaborative learning.

To start planning an essay, she helps each writer spell out voice, audience, and purpose on an overhead transparency while classmates give feedback:

> *JKT:* "Who would want to hear Carl tell how good he is in baseball?"
>
> *Class:* "A coach."
>
> *JKT:* "OK, why?"
>
> *Class:* "How about to convince him to give Carl a baseball scholarship. . . ."
>
> *JKT:* "Do you want to write to that audience, Carl?"

Now she meets with Darrell and his peer partner, Frank, for a conference. Usually reticent, Darrell has written a sensitive letter to the mother of his best friend. He reads aloud from a computer printout: "A friend is always there when you need him."

> *JKT:* "Good! Now how would you explain that to Bob's mother?"
>
> *Frank:* "He needs an example, like maybe going to pizza together."
>
> *JKT:* "Well, remember his purpose in writing to Bob's mother. So she'd be glad she raised a kid that other people would feel this way about. How about an example of a time that Bob was there for you. . . ."
>
> *Darrell:* "Well, like the time I was locked out."
>
> *JKT:* "What did Bob do?"
>
> *Darrell:* "Well, I went to his house and he let me in. And then he calmed me down and fixed me something to eat and then, you know, he let me spend the night."
>
> *JKT:* "Great! You know how many sentences you just said? Probably about five—and you need all of them in your paper. Would Bob's mother feel good to hear how her son treated you?"

Both boys nod, and Darrell jots down the new ideas on the back of his printout. Darrell is learning that he can talk his way through a draft, gaining fluency first, then using the computer to achieve a presentable final copy.

Many teachers who have used printouts in conference find they can coach their students to aim higher than they would dare expect with traditional writing tools. We can demand the mental hard work of revision because the physical act of revision is easy.

Projects and Publication

Clara McCrary (1981) crowns the revision process with publishing. Her background as a reading specialist shows in her classroom motto: "Every child an author." She began making the reading-writing connection before she ever touched a computer, by introducing African-American first graders to Langston Hughes.

McCrary would read aloud such poems as "Troubled Woman," and then guide her children to write such variants as "Troubled Dog" or "Troubled Brother and Me" (she contributed her own, "Troubled Teacher"). Her class published handwritten booklets of their own poetry modeled on Hughes. Listen as first graders respond to one of their favorites:

Baby[1]

Albert!
Hey, Albert!
Don't you play in dat road,
   You see dem trucks
   A goin' by.
   One run ovah you
   An' you die.
Albert, don't you play in dat road.

—Langston Hughes

Baby

Tene Hey Tene!
Stop rocking in that chair
You'll fall backards and bust your head
and maybe you might even be dead.
Tene Stop rocking in that chair.

—Tene Webb (age 6)

Baby

Hey Donnene, get up out of that bed

You sleepy head!
I don't want to get up and
do no work.
I like to sleep and stay in bed.
Yes, I'm a sleepy head.
Hey, Donnene, get up out of that bed,
You sleepy head!

—Donnene Fulton (age 6)

When she began working with computers, Clara McCrary quite naturally focused on publishing and literature. She found that word processing enabled children to produce writing in the same kind of print they were learning to read. The link between young authors and published authors became still more dramatic. Children liked to experiment with voice in their modeling: they intuitively aimed for standard English in their responses to "A Dream Deferred," while many played with dialect in their responses to "Baby." And their teacher found that the labor of revising a text they had struggled to transcribe became manageable even for primary students.

Next she developed her Langston Hughes project to include the poetry of other cultures, Native Americans and Jewish children of the Holocaust. She adapted the material for high school and adult basic writers, who also responded to the personal involvement in literature and to publishing their own verse. She finds the computer a natural support mechanism for an active reading program.

Like Clara McCrary, most of our teachers worked with writing before they discovered computers. Betty Barro journeyed in the opposite direction. She spent some years as a word-processing trainer; then she finished college, earned her certification, and began teaching English at Orchard Farm Middle School.

Barro was leading her rural district's writing inservice when the Missouri River flooded, closing the schools for two weeks. The teachers continued to meet at the public library. They decided to take what they had learned about the writing process back to their classrooms with an oral history project. For a week after school reopened, students throughout Orchard Farm wrote about the flood as they had experienced it. They documented the flood's impact on the community, recording their data from interviews and observations in handwritten journals.

Then they began revising their drafts on the computers. Barro rolled all fifteen of the middle school computers into her classroom for the project. A typing class recopied articles from schools which did not yet have computer access. The students' work was published in booklets and displayed at a districtwide Young Authors' Conference. The St. Louis *Post-Dispatch* used selections in a feature story about the flood.

Of course, the Orchard Farm teachers could have done an oral history without computers. However, Betty Barro is convinced that the new tools reinforced a process approach to writing:

> When the first luster of writing about their own flood experiences waned, the computer kept them on task. It motivated students to get the story done and into publication. My eighth graders often bog down after a first draft, and that's when I plug in the computers.

Asenath Lakes teaches at Beaumont High School in St. Louis, where few students are planning for college and most have family incomes below the poverty line. Publishing with computers is the heart of her program to motivate and challenge her writers. Lakes guides her students through the writing process in a well-equipped IBM lab. Peer response and conferencing lead to reasonably finished papers, graphics software makes easy-but-impressive covers, and the best papers compete for banners and certificates—produced, again, with graphics software.

Observe Beaumont High during the annual "Golden Caduceus Awards Assembly." Writers, wearing robes in the school colors, appear on stage to be honored with trophies in such categories as "best science paper explaining a process" or "best persuasive essay—social studies." Afterward, they attend a taped "press conference" where they answer questions about their winning papers, which are displayed for writers from the community. Publishing with the computer validates student writing and strengthens the commitment to the processes of writing.

Developing Curriculum

This commitment to process is the key to curriculum development for a WritingLand. Regardless of their backgrounds, most of our teachers first plan a writing program and then consider how to adjust their style or schedule to word processing. Developing a curriculum for writing with computers is not much different from developing any good writing process curriculum. But a few special techniques can be shared.

Sharon Franklin and Jon Madian (1988) suggest an easy way to prepare lesson files on disk. Some word-processing programs designed for schools let instructors type their material in a form that students can read but cannot change. "Template" or "frozen text" can be used again and again, just like a ditto master. But unlike a question typed on paper, frozen text leaves a space that can expand or shrink as students respond in natural language. On a printout, the frozen text with the teacher's instructions and background readings will be omitted. Frozen text works with prewriting or organizing or modeling activities— anything a teacher can write that prompts students to build and manipulate their own responses.

For young writers, choose a pattern story or poem to type with your word processor. Intersperse the literature with questions to help students read actively, reflect, and predict. During the guided reading lesson, students work with the patterns to model their own stories and poems. Then they print their original work—the teacher's text and the models stay frozen.

Teacher-made text files can also help students get "inside" a novelist's style. Try typing a few paragraphs from Hemingway with a word processor and then calling them up, a different passage on each screen. Ask each student to add just one sentence that Hemingway *might* have included in the passage. Tell the students to consider style as well as context, so that their new sentence flows seamlessly with the original. Then—either in hard copy or on the screen—show each passage of "enhanced" Hemingway to a different reader, who tries to identify the hoax.[2]

Word processing makes it easy to prepare sentence-combining lessons. You can type sets of kernel sentences from William Strong (1986) and ask students to develop their own combinations. They print, share their work in groups of four, and then decide on the best version for each set of kernels. One student working at the computer makes a revision representing the group's consensus.

When teachers realize that word processing is the essential all-purpose software for writers, they quickly start adapting their own best lessons and saving them on disk.

Shared Leadership, Shared Learning

Word processing can be a powerful tool in displaying the values of a writing community. All text is tentative, fluid. Writers—students and faculty—work together to experiment, to create, to evaluate, to play with language. And when the process is complete, writers celebrate their best work. The computer supports conferencing, revision, publication, and shared leadership in a WritingLand.

Anne Wright has coordinated the Hazelwood West writing lab for four years, introducing dozens of colleagues and students to word processing. I have shown how the computer reinforces our present goals in teaching the processes of writing. This teacher goes a step further by identifying ten ways the computer tends to change how we teach those processes (Wright 1988, 33–38). I'll summarize her list:

1. *Teachers become more flexible.* "I haven't heard of any schools that can provide classroom sets of computers," says Wright. Teachers share and take turns, adjusting the schedule of assignments and planning deadlines to make allowances for slower and faster typists. Many adjust their rules for final copy to match the format their printers can handle. In practice, teachers who aren't flexible don't wind up bringing their classes to the computer lab.

2. *Teachers learn word processing.* While most Hazelwood English teachers knew little about computers when the lab opened, those who continued bringing students are the ones who spent time becoming fluent with the new writing tools.

3. *Teachers require more revision.* Just typing a paper does not make it better. But since the computer makes changing a text so easy, teachers can require more extensive revision, and students no longer balk at multiple drafts.

4. *Students' improved attitudes toward revision affect instruction.* In fact, many who use the computer hesitate to turn in a "finished" paper: "But Mrs. Wright! I wanted to make some more changes!" For the first time, they are open to instruction in revising beyond the surface level—such as reorganizing large sections of text, or pruning severely.

5. *Composing is done mostly in class rather than as homework.* Before the computer, class time tended to be spent on prewriting and group editing activities. Now the actual drafting must be done in the lab.

6. *The peer editing process changes.* First, students in the lab spontaneously give and receive help as they write. Second, the structured peer response gets squeezed into homework time; students exchange drafts with a partner and record their feedback on a response guide. To retain the experience of reading papers aloud and building trust, Wright uses peer groups in class for handwritten papers and partner editing at home for papers drafted in the lab.

7. *Teachers learn to use computers for instruction.* A projector connected to a single computer brings to life this teacher's mini-

lessons on the composing process. She often "thinks aloud" while drafting or editing on the monitor, sharing with her classes how a skilled writer works through a paper. Students may then do sentence combining or paragraph revising on their individual computers.

8. *Experienced teachers give few computer instructions.* What writers really need to know about computers (indenting, deleting, word wrap) can be taught in about five minutes. "It took English teachers some time to learn that students could write without being experts at parsing sentences; it has likewise taken us some time to learn that they can do word processing without hours of computer instruction."

9. *Students spend more time on task, enabling teachers to help individuals.* Teachers take advantage of drafting time in the lab to give brief conferences. The computers help to support a serious-but-informal workshop atmosphere.

10. *Access affects student attitudes toward using computers.* When teachers sign up for a two-week block of time in the lab and go through the entire process of writing one paper, students quickly get comfortable with the computer. On the other hand, a short introduction to word processing followed by "sporadic, one-hour visits throughout the semester" may be a frustrating waste of time.

Many of the changes Anne Wright describes come only after we survive an uncomfortable time of adjustment. The arrival of new tools can be threatening, since most writing teachers learn the technology just a few steps ahead of their students. For some, the risk of appearing ignorant is too great. But for others, it's a new opportunity for teaching (Madigan and Sanders 1988).

For a technical writing course at the University of New Mexico, Chris Madigan designed a sequence of assignments to teach word processing inductively, along with technical writing forms. His classes of twenty-four students were working in a new lab with just twelve computers, limited access, and unfamiliar software. As they coped with these constraints, they compiled their short assignments into a major project: writing new, user-friendly documentation for their word-processing program.

Since the professor could not come across as the "expert," students took more responsibility for their own learning. They wrote for a real audience and purpose from an undeniable, felt need. Chris Madigan helped them analyze and describe each word processing function, but he couldn't supply well-written documentation. This kind of shared learning and leadership can be an unexpected benefit of teaching with computers.

Throughout this book I've been stressing that the computer is neither a teacher nor a cause of better writing. This chapter presents the flip side of these principles: the computer does, in fact, influence the way we write and the way we teach writing.

Notes

1. Copyright 1927 by Alfred A Knopf, Inc., and renewed 1955 by Langston Hughes. Reprinted from *Selected Poems of Langston Hughes,* by permission of the publisher.

2. This lesson is based on a presentation by Jon Madian at the February 1989 Midwest Technology Conference sponsored by the Regional Consortium for Education and Technology in St. Louis. I have varied it by choosing passages from a variety of fiction (Rudolfo Anaya's *Bless Me, Ultima;* James Baldwin's *Going to Meet the Man;* Margaret Laurence's *The Stone Angel;* N. Scott Momaday's *House Made of Dawn;* Toni Morrisson's *The Bluest Eye;* Henry David Thoreau's *Walden;* Kurt Vonnegut's *Slaughterhouse Five*), and by having students work in pairs at each computer to create their hoax sentences.

15 Peers

Managing Shared Authority

Whether or not they use computers, students are also teachers in a process-oriented writing class. Writers get feedback from peers as well as adults while they are developing their drafts. Perhaps you are already managing a writing workshop with response groups, peer tutoring, and collaborative composing. Perhaps your model for classroom interaction comes from the work of Bruffee (1983), Graves (1983) and the Johnsons (1988). But if you add computers, your writing workshop is likely to become still more student-centered.

Sometimes computers may lead to shared authority simply because the students know as much about them as their teachers. Maybe, in a few years, teacher-dominated writing classrooms will have computers as standard equipment. But for now, word processing lends itself to patterns of shared authority and feedback that have long been supported by writing process theory but are still often neglected in practice. Computer environments can be ideal, for example, to support peer tutoring, collaborative composing, and peer response.

Interaction often grows in a WritingLand, paradoxically, because students at the keyboard tend to remain on task. Georgia Schoeffel teaches in a St. Louis city high school where few of her colleagues use peer response or other group activities. They explain that group work is too noisy and makes classroom management more difficult. They saw another style of behavior when they brought their freshman classes to Schoeffel's lab for a demonstration writing lesson. Students helped one another with word-processing commands, checked word choice with the writer at the next keyboard, reviewed printouts with peer partners—all with low-voiced concentration.

In suburban Webster Groves, teachers on an action research team report similar success. They have found well-planned, cooperative learning the single most effective classroom strategy for low-skilled writers.

If you have tried group work with unsettling results, you may want to try it again in a computer writing environment.

Peer Tutoring

When first working with computers, teachers may really need assistance with such tasks as booting up, saving, and printing. Peer tutoring can be a natural way to build shared authority in a WritingLand.

Students who have computers at home are usually quick to volunteer their help as informal peer tutors. One problem with this is that your instant "experts" may be members of those racial or ethnic groups often identified as the privileged classes (Hawkins 1984; Mehan 1985). When encouraging peer assistance, be sure not to reinforce the inequities that already exist in society. If teachers recognize this danger, they can make the ad hoc computer aide a leadership role that is open to students who have not been able to excel in other ways. Watch what happened in one inner-city WritingLand on the day the computers arrived.

Six Apples and six printers were delivered in boxes to Langston Middle School, earmarked for the Writing Enrichment Lab. I offered to help the writing teacher assemble the equipment, although at the time I had never seen the inside of a computer.

Jackie Collier excused three eighth-grade boys from class, and together we tackled the first carton. I asked Derek to open the computer manual and read the first page of instructions while Bob and Lamont carried them out. (Feeling quite smug, I planned to have them switch roles for the next page, making the job an experience in real-world reading.)

For a moment I was surprised at how poorly all three boys read. After many visits to Collier's lab, I knew this slow, word-at-a-time reading was not typical. But my crew kept on reading—and they kept fitting cards into slots and cables into ports. Gradually, they came to recognize how the machine fit together and how the manual represented the machine. The students were thrilled when they finished their first computer and got to run an animated introduction to keys and commands.

The next day, their teacher told me that my three computer aides came from her special education class, all of them labeled "educable, mentally handicapped." She added that after I left the building, they had successfully put together a second computer almost entirely on their own. Later that day, when the service representative assembled the rest of the machines, he apparently didn't bother reading the second "update" to the manual. So the next morning, when the printer balked, Derek, Bob, and Lamont corrected the way he'd placed the printer card!

The enrichment lab's first computer "experts" were immeasurably proud of themselves. "Those three kids flew for weeks," Collier said. They would brag, "That's the one we put together. And that's the one the guy from Apple messed up." They quickly began teaching other students to connect the machines and boot up the word-processing software.

A new skill—one that "smart kids" don't already have—can empower academic "losers" with a second chance to succeed.

Emily Buckhannon, writing coordinator for suburban McCluer High School, has used this principle to organize another peer-tutoring program. She asks teachers to choose quiet, academically undistinguished kids to send for tutor-training. The tutors circulate around the computer lab, wearing badges. Their help is critical during the first and last ten minutes of a writing class, when they relieve the bottlenecks of booting up and saving files. In large classes, they can also stretch the limited hardware by freeing up a couple of workstations.

Watch as Lynda works in this setting with a couple of boys who were absent the previous day. She boots up their software, and as soon as they have a blank screen for writing, she slips back to her seat to continue her own paper. "Do you ever fall behind because you're helping other people?" She smiles. "Yeah, sometimes. But I like doing it." Lynda adds that she can catch up after school or during advisory period.

Peer tutoring can be a real help. Try consciously selecting your tutors in a way that counters stereotypes. Be sure to provide some individual training, showing them the lab's organization and equipment. Emily Buckhannon even lets them in on "dangerous secrets" (such as how to erase a whole page), thus giving them a sense of control in the new environment.

Encourage tutors to assist a writer, but not to take over the keyboard and show off for their classmates. They will learn how to teach by modeling what they see. Unlike experienced teachers, they're not already committed to a certain method, so they tend to learn quickly whatever you show them.

Collaborative Composing

Collaboration is one of the basic principles of any writing workshop. When writers work with computers, paired or group composing tends to become more common and more successful.

Some teachers began using collaborative activities to reduce computer anxiety and offer support for writers who were uneasy with the new tools. Others resorted to composing with a partner because of a shortage of hardware or supervision in the lab. Rochelle Ferdman had twenty-five children and twelve computers. Given a choice of either sending half her fifth graders to the lab alone or having them pair up at the keyboards, she chose the latter and quickly built up her repertoire of collaborative lessons.

But after trying it as an expedient, many of us have come to value collaborative composing for its own sake. It helps writers grow more aware of their own composing processes (Bruffee 1983). It also introduces students to a context that is typical of business and professional writing. In their large-scale survey, Bernhardt and Applebee (1985) show that such writing tasks as research reports, journal articles, curriculum proposals, and market analyses tend to be the work of joint authors. With computers, two or three students can each draft a section of a report, and then merge files and revise for continuity and style. The team talks and argues through the whole process.

It is true that collaborative composing can be difficult for some writers. After a few teachers in a Gateway institute chose to collaborate on research for their presentations, and loved the experience, I thought that everyone should try it. The next summer, teachers signed up for topics, three to a team. Each group shared the research and wrote a collaborative review on the computer. I was stunned by the contrasts in process and product. For teams who jelled, collaborative research was exciting; for teams whose learning styles, work habits, or writing styles were incompatible, the need to collaborate was torture.

Puzzling over what went wrong, I realized that my teams didn't get much time to work together and build trust before the pressure of a major assignment. Perhaps, too, they needed the option of working independently. Some writers, like Mary and Linda (chapter 3), collaborate spontaneously; most writers can *learn* to collaborate. But a few, especially those who are very advanced or very weak, seem to work better alone. (Both Youssef and Bob prefer to draft individually and then get peer response.)

To help writers get started with collaborative research, try this brief, in-class simulation. Students receive four clippings that discuss a recent news event in various ways—detailed facts, opinions, comparison with related stories, place in history. At each computer, partners first collaborate on a clear, one-paragraph summary of one article. They read their summaries aloud to check comprehension and to see the differences between what they saw as important and what others chose.

Then each pair drafts a short journalistic piece that draws from all four clippings. First discuss the task. Writers will eventually see that they need to come up with an "angle," a point of their own to which they can link the data from the clippings. They invariably run into problems, so the articles go through much debate and revision before finding a focus. And when the partners share aloud, the audience is startled to hear the diversity of treatments based on the same material.

This mini-lesson in collaboration highlights the real challenge of research writing: not footnotes, not bibliography, but synthesis. Researchers must weave together data from different sources and use it for their own purpose in a text with the voice of a writer, not a committee.

Peer Response

It sounds like a wonderful idea for students to help each other revise and edit their writing. Peers gain experience in critical reading while the teacher gains some allies in responding to the paper load. But the results are often disappointing.

In 1977, after taking a seminar with James Britton, I eagerly set up peer groups in my college classes. The freshmen read aloud, listened to their classmates, and generally tried to humor me, but in most cases the best writers simply rewrote everyone else's papers. At the end of the semester, the course evaluations told what my students thought: "She's a very nice teacher, but she should quit experimenting on her students with her newfangled ideas from graduate school!" Since I'm very stubborn, I didn't "quit," but I did learn that peer response must be taught.

Joan Krater [Thomas] (1981) models the process for her eighth graders by choosing one paper for whole-class response. She makes a photocopy for each student and also projects a transparency on the overhead. (She chooses a paper with some strong elements as well as a clear need for improvement.) Revisions are recorded on the overhead as students discuss the paper and mark up their individual copies.

Through this approach, writers gradually learn to edit with less guidance. After going through the sample paper on the transparency, each student selects a short passage to revise individually for a unified effect; these revisions are dittoed and discussed in class. Next, students choose a passage from one of their own previous papers, and each member of the peer group attempts a revision. The group compares their versions and writes a final revision collaboratively.

After this sequence of guided revision lessons, the students' drafts became "messier, revisions became more substantial, peer groups became more effective, and [they] took a major step toward becoming better writers" (46).

Anne Wright's lessons that use the computer linked to the large monitor work in much the same way. The teacher first guides and models peer feedback with the whole class, and then sends writers off to review papers in their small writing groups. In both cases, the key to successful peer feedback is preparing the peers.

Students *learn* how to respond through experiencing their teacher's response in whole-class sharing and in individual conferences. It helps to make explicit the theme and the form of response. Rochelle Ferdman's elementary writers take turns sitting in the big "author's chair" to read aloud. The class discussion follows set guidelines: (1) "What did you hear?" (brief summary of the writing), and (2) "What questions do you have?" (ideas for development, clarification, and polishing). These same guidelines, posted on the wall, are used by teachers for conferences and by students for peer response.

Most writers learn to respond constructively to content and style sooner than they learn to edit and proofread accurately. Watch Carol Henderson teaching her fourth and fifth graders to edit mechanical errors with a paired activity in the lab. She gives her instructions briskly: "The person on the right is the writer; the person on the left is the editor. Right is writer, left is editor. We are going to be checking for capitalization, spelling, and punctuation." The children nod—they know the "sentence game." Their teacher dictates, "Today is Monday, January 9, 1989." Each student on the right keys in the sentence. Then the peer on the left makes corrections, although both partners talk their way through the editing decisions.

If a team asks for help, Henderson gives a cue that directs their attention toward the error: "Jamal and Terrill, you have a punctuation problem." Her style of guided inquiry in editing shows the influence of Shaughnessy (1977) and Hull (1985): the point is not simply to avoid an error, but to think through it to a real grasp of the standard forms. When a team is finished, she types "right" or "wrong" at the end of their sentence and briefly conferences with them on what they missed. The children, too, continue discussing their versions: "I *knew* it had to be punctuation here for the 'S' to be capital, Dodo!" Teams getting three out of five sentences "right" win special pencils.

In my own class of prospective English teachers, I use a single computer to model a specific editing dilemma: sexist usage. We talk about the fact that usage is not a fixed grammatical law but a changing matter of social convention. We talk about the dilemma of today's writer, who must often choose between sounding sexist, awkward, or ungrammatical. I urge them as professionals to try using nonsexist forms in their curriculum work and give them the NCTE guidelines for nonsexist usage. And then their papers arrive: "The student will share his/her draft with his/her peers, after which he/she will revise for publication." Help!

Typing a few stylistic atrocities on disk, I display them on the big monitor and ask students to propose revisions in graceful English. Although the same samples could be shown on an overhead, the beauty of using the computer is that we can play with revisions— experimenting, laughing, applauding—until we find an acceptable version. The lesson helps teachers become more sophisticated, sensitive critics and editors.

The dynamics of a WritingLand are complex. The next chapter pulls together the elements I've been discussing—time, space, equipment, teachers, and peers—to propose an overall design.

16 Designing a WritingLand

Planning a computer-equipped environment for writers makes me feel like a mapmaker in the Age of Exploration—I sit by candlelight, drafting maps based on travelers' reports of a New World with its fabled Seven Cities of Gold. And some distant conquistador will trudge the desert, map in hand, searching for the gold amid the hostile elements.

The WritingLand is still too new for consensus. We lack a shared history, recognized boundaries, established laws. At the same time, getting lost in places that aren't user-friendly can be expensive.

Here are a few landmarks that schools have found helpful in designing a WritingLand.

Priorities: Teachers before Tools

In your budget, the one essential item is good teaching. Better to plan a really fine classroom with a dozen computers and a full-time writing teacher than to invest in thirty machines and a program that is too big to monitor. Be sure that there will be skilled support available while students are actually composing at the computer.

Think of how the computer can enhance the way you want to teach writing. For example, the computer can aid collaboration, ease revision, and lead to professional-looking publications. It motivates reluctant writers. Plan your program keeping in mind these features of writing instruction, and let the computer help you. Avoid or minimize lessons that simply introduce the computer or teach a software application. These are the electronic counterparts of what Britton and others (1975) call "dummy run" papers, like the paragraphs written simply to show that one can write a paragraph. Instead, provide the human support to teach writing well—assisted by the computer wherever it is a genuine asset.

Train Peer Tutors and Aides

You can increase that support by training a few students and paraprofessionals. These people need to know how to use the hardware

147

and software, how to solve common technical problems, and how to give support to writers in process.

Several times, I've observed classes in settings where two official helpers were giving different messages. As students typed a first draft, their writing teacher was saying, "Nice details—tell me more," or "I'm getting confused here. Can you spell out how we get from that idea to this one?" At the same time the aide or untrained classroom teacher was saying, "Watch your spelling," and "I can't believe these children make so many mistakes!" Writers need consistent cues on what issues to deal with first.

To prevent this conflict, plan a tutoring workshop. You might model the program on National Writing Project courses, with time for the tutors to do some of their own writing and to give and receive feedback.

Plan a Schedule

In some schools, a small lab has such demand for access that each student rarely touches a computer. In others, a new lab sits empty for much of the day; teachers with already packed schedules don't see how the computer fits into their curriculum.

It helps if one person who is on-site—a writing center director or librarian—takes charge of the schedule. To defuse any resentment, include the whole staff in decisions on access. Teachers, if consulted, may be willing to give a few colleagues most of the lab time at first. These people can develop a pilot plan for computers and writing. When they report back, the schedule and access can be revised to include more classes.

Ideally, the center will be staffed by professional writing teachers. One or two may share the leadership, or a group of teachers may be released one period per day to staff the facility. If you choose the second plan, our experience suggests that one person should be the director, who is given an extra administrative hour to keep records and prepare materials such as a lab manual or tutor's handbook (Brooks 1989).

Don't Skimp on Space

Remember that a writing workshop needs more space than a computer-programming lab. Ignoring the protests of the efficiency experts, negotiate for the largest possible room. Allow enough space for writers to spread out drafts, to move around, and to conference with peers and teacher.

You can increase the space that is actually available to writing classes by placing your WritingLand near a library or learning center. Design ways for people and activities to flow from the computer environment to other settings. Enlist the help and suggestions of librarians, media directors, and others responsible for the adjacent territory. If you can't plan a lab that will accommodate a whole writing class, plan for a cluster or suite of facilities, each with appropriate support for writers.

Start with a Flexible Design

As you develop a WritingLand, your plan will probably need several revisions. Avoid the sort of architectural changes that are hard to undo. First, get to know through experience what layout and equipment you really want.

Steger Sixth Grade Center in Webster Groves built a small lab based entirely on rolling carts. Each computer sits on a standard-height desk with wheels, and the desks fit together smoothly, creating two full walls of computers. Teachers first assumed they would often borrow a machine and roll it into their classrooms. They found this wasn't practical, since someone generally wanted to bring a class to a functioning lab; besides, undoing the cables took too much time. Now they simply keep one whole workstation sitting on a taller audiovisual cart and ready to travel.

But a flexible design in a pilot lab makes long-range planning and revision simpler. When the school wants to invest in a larger lab, equipment can be moved intact, without damage either to the workstations or to the original lab room.

Visit a WritingLand

The teachers and administrators from a school that is planning a new facility should do some first-hand research. The most effective research is also the simplest: go to see the best labs and computer classrooms in your area. Some computer-equipped writing programs have been recognized as NCTE Centers of Excellence, making them natural sites for such demonstrations. As you visit WritingLands, you will make new contacts with computer-wise educators who can be helpful in the future. Then, after taking another look at your own school setting and needs, you can adapt the models.

Another kind of modeling can happen within a school. If one teacher is already knowledgeable about writing with computers, that staff member can be the catalyst for others. Sometimes this happens informally, as teachers talk and visit after school. More often, it takes deliberate planning. If the writing specialist has some released time, colleagues can visit the lab with their classes and take part in demonstration lessons. They will see a process approach to teaching writing in action and in the setting that they, too, will use. As an alternative the program can be demonstrated through an inservice workshop.

Sponsor a Schoolwide Inservice Workshop

If your computer writing facility will serve the whole English department (or the whole school), why not celebrate its arrival with a workshop?

The "writing process" has become such a cliché that in many schools it's hard to get experienced teachers to come to an inservice workshop. "I've done that" may simply refer to a few hours of staff development and the oversimplification of process found in most student texts. But without a felt need to learn more, most of us will leave well enough alone.

The computer is a wonderful creator of that "felt need." Be sure the workshop teaches the computer indirectly by demonstrating good writing lessons and helping teachers compose their own short papers at the keyboard. Keeping the writing light and personal will reduce stress and computer anxiety. Conclude the workshop by publishing a booklet of the teachers' writing, illustrated with graphics software. An inservice of twenty to thirty contact hours should prepare staff for a WritingLand.

A fringe benefit is that a good inservice will increase the sense of community among writing teachers. It gives them permission to ask one another for help with lessons and with equipment, fostering the shared authority that will be developing in classes where computers support a process approach to writing.

Work with Your Administrators

Teachers can spend the summer at a writing institute and return to school full of enthusiasm for teaching writing with computers—only to find they can't get access to the lab, and the computers have been dedicated to a new drill-and-practice program. Because several participants suffered experiences like this, the Gateway Writing Project requires all applicants to have an administrator's endorsement and a letter describing how their training will be put to use. Support from the top is essential to a WritingLand.

Talk with principals, department chairs, computer and curriculum coordinators. Let colleagues know what you know. Be sure that strong writing teachers have leading roles on the committees that design your writing center. Decisions about scheduling, access, layout, staffing, software and hardware require the joint planning of teachers and administrators.

The next chapters look in more detail at leadership, staff development, and "Writing Improvement Teams" in schools which emphasize writing with computers.

Map Your WritingLand

Figure 10 (see chapter 5) pulls together the key elements in designing a WritingLand. As a map it can serve as a guide and reminder as you plan an environment for writing with computers. Or you might map your own WritingLand based on your understanding of its dynamics.

What I see is a network of processes. The *writing process* puts planning, translating, and reviewing in a context of oral language, which is monitored by a whole person who thinks, feels, relates, and remembers. The *instructional process* may begin with a rhetorical problem and involve mini-lessons in prewriting, drafting, and editing with feedback. The *environmental process* includes the interaction of teacher, peers, and administrators, and tools available for writing and publishing, decisions on time, space, and access, and also the views of society on the roles of writing and of computers. The *staff development process*, which may have prompted the whole design, is seen as a continuing source of learning.

Designing a WritingLand is itself a process of composition, so it takes planning and revisions, as well as collaboration, to create a successful one.

IV Who Rules a WritingLand?

17 Administrators

A teacher can return from a process-oriented workshop, close the classroom door, and quietly change an accustomed approach to writing instruction. But the changes tend to be short-lived unless they meet with some support beyond the classroom.

Several years ago, I surveyed everyone who had completed the Gateway Writing Project's summer invitational institute. The teachers had returned to give ten hours of workshops in the writing process to their colleagues at school. I asked what changes the Project had made in their own teaching, and what impact, if any, their participation had made on their schools. The results seemed puzzling at first.

Their answers ranged from *great impact* ("my whole department has been transformed; we do peer response, holistic assessment, young authors' conferences, everything") to *little or no impact* ("the school is pushing for mastery learning, and I'm running off dittos to hit all the objectives"). Studying the surveys, I noticed that one factor kept emerging when teachers tried to explain a positive impact: the school administrator. One memorable comment: "My principal is a former English teacher, so he understands!"

Good administrators are the power behind good school writing programs. Here are some ways they can use that power[1]:

Funding: They obtain the funds to support writing tools, centers, activities, and improvement. Solid funding is necessary to bring about most of the next seven items.

Reasonable Teaching Loads: For years, the National Council of Teachers of English has urged a maximum of a hundred students for teachers of writing, a goal seldom reached except in schools with strongly committed administrators.

Schedules: They plan schedules which support writing teachers. Fragmented class periods with frequent interruptions are not conducive to a writing workshop.

Teacher Evaluation and Feedback: Good administrators recognize and reward good teaching of writing. They give the supportive feedback that encourages teachers to grow.

155

Inservice Programs: Good administrators resist the scattershot approach to staff development, and they sponsor programs with the intensity to have an impact. Then they show their support by participating in the workshops.

Peer Coaching: Administrators can provide a structure to help teachers of writing observe one another, model new techniques, give and receive feedback. Mentoring should be supportive rather than evaluative and linked to the inservice program.

Writing Assessment: Good administrators can insist on testing that includes whole pieces of discourse. Holistic evaluation of papers is a start, along with portfolio assessment and other measures of the full writing process.

Writing Across the Curriculum: They do not regard writing as the sole responsibility of the English department. And they urge teachers of other subjects to do more for writing improvement than to count off for spelling errors.

Administrators play a key role in any school writing program. They play an even more crucial role in writing programs that involve computers. In most schools, the major decisions on software and hardware purchases, lab layout, scheduling, staffing, and access are made by administrators.

A WritingLand cannot succeed without knowledgeable and supportive leaders. Administrators need to understand the basics of teaching the writing process. They need to understand what computers can—and cannot—do to improve writing. Finally, they need to understand team leadership, so that their plans for a computer-equipped writing program can change and grow with the insights of writing teachers and technical experts. (More on "Writing Improvement Teams" in the next chapter.)

What One Principal Did

Cindy Jaskowiak understands WritingLands from two different perspectives. As an English teacher, she worked with Anne Wright to direct the computer-equipped writing lab at Hazelwood West High School. A few years later, as a principal, she worked to rebuild the writing program at Lindbergh High School.

Until Jaskowiak arrived, Lindbergh was a fairly typical middle-class, midwestern suburban high school. The English department was a collection of strong but diverse personalities. Two teachers had studied with the Gateway Writing Project, and one of them taught writing courses for the university. The department chair, who had a fine background in literature, emphasized college preparation through reading and analyzing major works. Each member of the department seemed to have a different focus; a shared philosophy about writing was lacking.

The next chapter will take a closer look at what Lindbergh's Writing Improvement Team accomplished in just two years. But the catalyst that put the process in motion was the principal.

When Cindy Jaskowiak arrived, she asked each department what changes they wanted to see. The English teachers asked for smaller classes to support instruction in writing. The principal was willing, provided that smaller class size went along with overall curriculum revision based on a departmentwide inservice program. The staff agreed. This principal's leadership brought the department together; teachers gave their full cooperation because they would gain the smaller classes they wanted. The result was a striking flow of energy, dialogue, and constructive planning that has revitalized the Lindbergh English department.

How Administrators Can Make a WritingLand Prosper

Allan Glatthorn's classic guide (1981) shows how administrators can improve writing through staff development, clinical observation, writing assessment, curriculum reform, and writing across the curriculum.

Glatthorn stresses that an administrator must know what a good writing classroom looks like before trying to observe and evaluate a writing teacher. (Remember the principal who visited a class where children sat in groups sharing their drafts, working on independent reading, or conferencing individually; the principal frowned slightly, then whispered to the teacher, "I'll come back on a day when you're teaching.")

A WritingLand environment doesn't look like a lecture class. It usually looks more like an art room or a science lab— students busy with a variety of tasks and teachers moving about as needed. When computers are an integral part of the writing program, the landscape differs still more from a conventional "English" classroom. And if the lab has been designed for writers, it won't look like a conventional computer lab, either. Videotapes of process-centered writing classes can help supervisors revise their thinking and modify their expectations. Parkway South High School has a video of their Center of Excellence writing lab, showing students writing at the computer and conferencing with staff.

The University of Missouri–St. Louis offers an annual one-day seminar, "Computers, Writing, and Effective Leadership." The keynote talk is given by a successful principal like Cindy Jaskowiak, with videotapes and presentations by Writing Improvement Teams.

For our leadership seminar, we have adapted parts of Glatthorn's book, now unfortunately out of print, to the special issues of computers and writing. Such materials highlight key elements of a process approach to teaching with old and new writing tools, as well as the active participation of peers and teacher in writing and responding. Figure 12 shows our version of a form supervisors can use to record a writing class visit.

Along with supervision, our seminar deals with the challenges of planning a WritingLand program. Team leadership should bring together school administrators, writing specialists, computer specialists, and media specialists. Unfortunately, the people who are knowledgeable about writing tend to have little contact with the people who are knowledgeable about computers.

This exercise will assess the situation in your own school: Brainstorm a list of "Computer Experts." Include the people who know a lot about computers and those whose jobs put them in a decision-making capacity. Now brainstorm a similar list of "Writing Experts." Whose names appear on both lists? Share with the group the *roles* of people who share both areas of expertise. Consider what kinds of staff development might bring about more integration of computers and writing.

The seminar stresses the importance of the physical environment. The presenters first describe (and draw) several lab arrangements. Then we survey the group, asking how computers are arranged in their own buildings. We find that the most common design is the small lab with twelve to eighteen computers set in straight, tight rows. Most schools do not have a regular procedure for making informed decisions on computer-equipped writing programs and settings.

Another issue new to many administrators is the impact of technology on equity. Computers in schools may decrease—or increase—the gap between mainstream and disadvantaged groups. As a member of the FIPSE Technology Study Group (FTSG 1988), I worked closely with some imaginative programs for women, minority groups, rural students, and others who may be isolated from technology and power. FTSG's policy statement concludes that "access alone does not insure equity" (50). Students who have computers at home will show more

WRITING WORKSHOP OBSERVATION

Teacher _____ Date _____

Course and Location _____

Observer _____

WRITING PROCESS SKILLS

Prewriting, such as—
    Thinking/discussing
    Oral/written planning
    Data gathering
    Voice/audience

Drafting, such as—
    Organization
    Sentence structure
    Word choice
    Leads/conclusions
    Paragraph development

Editing, such as—
    Spelling
    Standard usage
    Manuscript form
    Publishing

Interaction, such as—
    Collaborative writing
    Peer feedback
    Teacher conference
    Other audience response

TOOLS AND MATERIALS USED

Such as—
Pen/pencil/paper   Black/whiteboard
Computer/software   Publishing/art supplies
    (Word processing,   Reference soures
    graphics, database)   Textbooks (specify)

Fig. 12. Writing workshop observation form. (Adapted from: *Writing in the Schools: Improvement through Effective Leadership* by Allan A. Glatthorn, pp. 59–62. Copyright 1981 by NASSP. Used with permission.)

WRITING WORKSHOP OBSERVATION—p. 2

Teacher _____ Date _____

WHAT TEACHER DOES   **WHAT STUDENTS DO**
(Describe activities)   (Describe activities)

Prewriting

Drafting

Editing

Interaction

Overall Impression and Comments:

Fig. 12. *Continued.*

sophistication in the lab at school; this is why we suggest choosing less obvious candidates as peer tutors. A subtle, but greater, risk is that computer applications will differ in courses for "haves" and "have-nots." College-bound students may be doing computer programming and word processing (where they will learn to master the computer), while basic students are doing drill and practice (where the computer will program the learner). Such contrasting applications may "track certain groups into passive relationships with technology" and "cripple the development of creative and self-empowering abilities" (51).

In our leadership seminar, we discuss the FTSG study. Then we report the research: ironically, basic writers are the ones who most consistently make progress in composing original texts on the computer. Schools should plan computer access to support this potential for progress.

For a WritingLand to prosper, we must pull together these diverse human and physical resources. Administrators have found the inventory in figure 13 helpful. This inventory can be used in various ways. During our seminar, administrators begin to fill out the inventory. Later, they go back to their buildings to consult with the necessary people to complete the planning process.

The inventory is also used during the last week of Gateway Writing Project summer institutes, when each teacher invites an administrator to attend. On visiting day, teachers from the same building work through the questions with their administrators and begin to form a Writing Improvement Team. They design a one-year action plan based on the best pooled knowledge available to them.

A Writing Improvement Team changes what Andrea Herrmann (1989) calls the "traditional hierarchy of power" in schools (117–18):

> Administrators and teachers need to work together collaboratively. Without effective collaboration with teachers, principals may find them unwilling to acquire the necessary computer skills or fearful of trying new approaches in their classrooms. Administrators will also fail to benefit from the teachers' specialized knowledge, namely their subject-matter expertise. . . . Collaboration means that teachers will no longer be excluded from the decision-making process. A committee of computer-using teachers should always be included in formulating decisions that affect them.

Such team leadership makes building a WritingLand possible. The next chapter will look in some detail at the work of Writing Improvement Teams formed in several schools with the help of the Gateway Writing Project.

**GATEWAY WRITING PROJECT,
UNIVERSITY OF MISSOURI–ST. LOUIS
COMPUTERS AND WRITING PROGRAM INVENTORY**

Staff Knowledge of Composing Processes

Which teachers have participated in a writing project or other intensive study in writing? When?

Has your building or district sponsored a writing inservice? When? How many contact hours? How many people?

Which teachers are recognized as writing experts by colleagues?

Who is responsible for curriculum and staff development in *writing?* (Principal, instructional coordinator, English department chair)

Staff Knowledge of Computers

Which teachers have been trained to use computers through university, technology center, or school programs?

Which teachers are recognized as computer experts by colleagues?

Which teachers use word processing with their writing classes?

Who is responsible for software purchases and staff development in *computers?*

Assess your needs for staff development in writing and in computers:

Computer Resources

Computers available to writing students in your building? Kind & number _____

Printers? Kind & number _____

Word-processing software? Programs _____

Other software useful to writers: _____

Class sets of blank disks? _____

Fig. 13. Writing improvement team inventory form.

Plans for purchase within 1 year: _____

Assess your needs for hardware and software acquisition:

Setting

Where do (will) students write with computers? (Writing lab, computer lab, library media center, English classroom, other)

Which staff member is in charge of this facility? (Writing teacher, computer/media/other teacher, aide, parent, no regular staffing)

Is a classroom teacher present as students write with computers?

What other support is available? (e.g., student tutors)

Analyze your computer setting. Are computers in rows or around the periphery? Is there space on the workstations to spread out materials? Is there space away from the computers for peer groups, conferencing, individual seating? Draw your setting:

Assess your needs for improved setting and support:

Access and Equity

How often does each writing student have access to computers?

Do certain groups of students have priority? (Grade levels? Subject areas? Gifted? Basic?)

Compare the computer applications used by college-bound and basic students. Is one group learning word processing and programming while the other is limited to computerized drill?

Are the computers used more/differently by students of one sex? One race? Is there a system in place to promote equity?

Fig. 13. *Continued.*

Which students assist with the computers? Is this arranged by individual teachers, or is there an official school program for training them? How are tutors selected?

What changes should be made in access priorities and curriculum to assure equity?

Writing Improvement Team

WHO?   Building administrators:

Skilled writing teachers:

Teachers from other departments:

Librarian, computer coordinator, etc.:

Outside resources (writing project, technology center, district experts, university consultants):

WHEN?   Common planning time? How often?

WHERE? Place for team planning meetings?

WHY?   Incentives, support for participants? (e.g., released time)

The Next Step . . .

Working together as a Writing Improvement Team, develop an action plan for the next year.

Fig. 13. *Continued.*

Notes

1. This list was suggested by Allan Glatthorn. In his letter of March 21, 1989, Professor Glatthorn commented on a draft of this chapter and gave permission to adapt his material from *Writing in the Schools: Improvement through Effective Leadership* (Arlington, VA: NASSP, 1981). Permission has also been granted by the publisher.

18 Writing Improvement Teams

The boundaries of a WritingLand extend far beyond the lab or publishing center. After an extensive review of programs and research, Gail Hawisher (1989) noted:

> The introduction of computers into English curricula is a contextual change that encourages and brings about alterations in the political, social, and educational structures of an entire system. Research that attempts to identify the influences of computers on an English department or an entire school is sorely needed. (62)

Designing a successful computer-assisted writing program requires teamwork on the part of administrators, writing teachers, computer specialists, and other resource people. Such teams need ready access to new information as the technology continues to develop. Here is how the Gateway Writing Project defines a Writing Improvement Team:

Staff:

One or more building administrators who completed the leadership seminar.

One lead teacher who completed the full Writing Project institute.

One or (preferably) more team teachers who completed shorter workshops in writing/computers.

Resource members as appropriate (library/media specialist, computer coordinator, lab aide, subject area leaders).

Team Needs:

Power to make decisions on computer-equipped writing program: curriculum, equipment, physical setting, staff development.

Common planning time for regular meetings.

Access to current knowledge through colleges, writing projects, technology centers, industry representatives, or staff development programs.

Our project has been working with schools since 1984 to build Writing Improvement Teams. The process includes the leadership seminar for administrators, courses and follow-up meetings for teachers, the WIT inventory (chapter 17, figure 13), and staff visits to teams at several pilot schools.[1] As a site visitor, I've come to see what problems tend to emerge as a school integrates computers into the writing program and what strategies within the school tend to resolve those problems.

Let's look again at Lindbergh High School. When Principal Cindy Jaskowiak first called for an overhaul of the writing program, the English department decided to work with the Gateway Writing Project. In the past, the department chair's focus had been literature, with writing occurring mainly in the form of critical essays. But when Jim Conway agreed to revamp the writing curriculum, he committed himself to the task without reservation: "I've read the new Core Competencies list and the state is mandating writing process. That means our kids are going to be tested on it and we're going to be teaching it more. My job is to see that we know how to do it well."

He went on to lead a Writing Improvement Team which included the principal, two teachers who were Gateway-trained, and one teacher new to a process approach. During the next two years, the team implemented a substantial inservice course, informal peer coaching and observation, schoolwide writing assessment, and steps toward writing across the curriculum.

Inservice Programs

The essence of Jim Conway's leadership style comes across in the role he assumed during Lindbergh's twenty-hour inservice. I'd asked if he, as department chair, would like to team-teach the workshop with a Gateway-trained presenter from another school. "Of course not!" he replied. "I need to take the course myself—but I'll be there writing at every session." And he was. Their leader's willingness to become a learner had a powerful impact on others in the department.

Lindbergh's teachers came together during that inservice. Sharing, laughing, struggling, and editing, they published a book of personal writing and a book of curriculum strategies (the latter was printed, spiral-bound, and distributed to every teacher in the school).

To prepare a Writing Improvement Team, we recommend a writing-centered workshop of twenty to thirty contact hours. Shorter programs tend to be awareness sessions, showcasing ideas but not providing the skills to make them work in the classroom.

The workshop can be planned as an intensive course during the week or two before the school year opens, or as a more extensive course offered on Saturdays or in late afternoons and spread over several months. In either case, our workshops follow a model familiar to people from any National Writing Project site. Teachers take on the role of students in their writing classes, participating in guided pre-writing, drafting, peer response, editing, and publishing. If the writing program is to incorporate computers, teachers do their writing at the keyboard.

Throughout the workshop, we use a two-pronged approach. Teachers first experience some aspect of writing, and then step back to reflect on that experience and how it applies to their teaching. Theory and practice come together. Sally Reagan (1988) notes that just as we tell our writing students, "Show, don't tell," we must "show" good classroom techniques rather than "tell" about them in workshops for teachers.

Peer Coaching, Mentoring, and Observation

When the Lindbergh Writing Improvement Team started to plan, they considered linking their inservice to better use of the computer lab for writing. But their priority was to show teachers a process approach to writing and how to teach and evaluate it. They feared the computer might upstage the writing if the workshop tried to deal with both agendas.

Their decision produced an unexpected result: a formal inservice with computers has not been needed. Three English teachers were already making extensive use of the lab and understood how to integrate computers in a process approach to teaching. They had been using these skills in isolation. Now, the Writing Improvement Team opened lines of communication between teachers who didn't usually share ideas. People began asking John Weiss how to do word processing and how to work with classes in the lab. Sometimes they came to the lab during their planning periods to observe him. Sometimes he volunteered to help them with their first class.

This process of informal mentoring was encouraged by the administration. After the writing inservice, Cindy Jaskowiak asked teachers to pick a colleague with whom they felt comfortable working. They began visiting one another's classes to reinforce what they had learned. Someone who had used a process approach for years might pair up with a teacher who was new to the process approach. Using their preparation periods, each teacher would observe the other's writing lesson and provide feedback. Teachers who chose to do this paired observation found it to be a very supportive experience.

Research on peer coaching, notably that of Joyce and Showers (1988), has identified several criteria for success:

1. Coaching programs are *"attached to training programs.* Coaching relationships continue and extend training in the workplace as trainees attempt to master and implement new knowledge, skills, and strategies."

2. Coaching develops a "community of learners engaged in the *continuous* study of teaching, curriculum, and academic content."

3. Since formal staff development cannot spell out the best ways to apply new techniques in each classroom context, "coaching is *experimental* in nature."

4. To provide a safe, supportive climate for experiment and study, "coaching relationships are completely *separate from supervision and evaluation"* (84–85).

Table 6, based on the Joyce and Showers's model of adult learning, suggests why a Writing Improvement Team can be a more powerful source of change than out-of-context workshops and outside consultants. In the latter forms of training, a learner hears about, observes, or perhaps even tries out the target behavior in a safe environment that's separate from everyday activities. The problem comes when the learner tries to transfer the new skills to the real world, where people are distracting, equipment breaks down, and failures are more costly.

The only training method that avoids this transfer problem is "coaching in the workplace." A WIT can provide this sort of continuing support for teachers in the classroom setting.

"Acquiring unnatural behavior" isn't easy. When writing teachers try to change a system they have used for years and refined until it works smoothly, they have a right to some support. This is true whether or not the change involves new writing tools. Teachers should have access to knowledgeable help when they are stymied by a student's error patterns. They should be able to ask a colleague to observe their peer groups and help improve response. When computers enter the picture, the need for "coaching in the workplace" is even greater.

When Georgia Schoeffel returned to her St. Louis City high school from a writing process institute, her principal asked her to share the program with her colleagues. Most weren't using either a process approach or computers. Morale in the district was low, and there was no funding to pay teachers for their time. An after-school inservice seemed futile—few people would come, and even fewer would try computers with their students. The school's lab had no aide or technical expert to call in a crisis.

Instead, Principal Tom Daly gave his writing specialist two periods of released time to model her program "in the workplace." She planned a five-week unit that guided students through the processes of writing while introducing them to computers. She offered to teach this unit to any freshman communications class—provided the regular teacher would accompany the class and assist in the lab. The results? She inserviced almost every teacher in her department. The following year, about half of them continued to use the lab independently. Georgia Schoeffel became an inhouse consultant in writing and computers.

A Writing Improvement Team can be most effective if the members have some released time for mentoring. Other teachers start to rely on the team's leadership, knowing that if they try a new technique or a new computer application, they can find help. New ideas can disseminate naturally throughout the department.

And beyond. . . . The Writing Improvement Team should visit successful sites to observe other labs, other software, other teaching methods. This informal modeling, widespread in the St. Louis metropolitan area, is a new kind of dissemination fostered by the computer. Of course model programs have long been showcased for visitors, but when a school adopts a new curriculum or a new schedule, faculty don't normally get a half-day off to see it in action somewhere across the county. When a school plans a new lab, people know that bad decisions will be expensive to undo.

Writing Assessment

As their third task, the Lindbergh team planned a schoolwide writing assessment. Every student wrote an essay in class which would be scored holistically on a rubric that was designed by the teachers during the inservice. The principal and department chair handled the details of communicating with teachers, coding papers, and dedicating a staff work day for scoring. WIT member Mary Ann Fanter helped prepare a professional report with graphs showing the upward trend of scores across the grade spectrum. This report, like the curriculum book, was distributed throughout the school.

Notice the message that was getting across to other departments. Writing was a real priority that made important people invest commitment and energy and even money. (This message was remembered a year later when Lindbergh sponsored a writing-across-the-curriculum workshop.)

Table 6
Acquiring Unnatural Behavior

Strategies	Outcomes		
	Knowledge	Demonstrate the behavior	Transfer to work setting
Presentation of concepts and theory	85%	15%	10%
Demonstration of behavior	85%	18%	10%
Low-risk practice plus feedback	85%	80%	15%
Coaching in workplace re: behavior and decisions	90%	90%	80%

(Adapted from: *Student Achievement through Staff Development* by Bruce Joyce and Beverly Showers, p. 71. Copyright 1988 by Longman Publishing Group. Reprinted by permission of Longman Publishing Group.)

In working with schools, I have come to accept the fact that writing improvement is usually, at some level, assessment-driven. Whether it's the state competencies or the district essay test, assessment gets people in motion. A Writing Improvement Team can best succeed when it works *with* writing evaluation. The first step is to make sure the assessment product is a full piece of discourse (not multiple-choice answers). The second step is to make sure the assessment process fits the instruction in writing. For example, many schools follow the procedures of the National Assessment of Educational Progress. NAEP gives students fifteen minutes to produce a writing sample; three prompts are addressed back-to-back in a total of forty-five minutes. James Gray, Director of the National Writing Project, comments[2]:

> When we promote the idea that writing can best be taught as a
> process, we are simply stating that student writers should be
> treated as writers, that they be given time to think about what
> they might write, time to try out an idea, time to revise, time to
> come up with a second draft if necessary, time to edit the final
> draft. [Real writers don't] sit down and knock off first and final
> copy in 15 minutes! Flaubert would have had a heart attack if
> forced to do what NAEP asks our students to do! I certainly would
> not want to have my writing abilities assessed under such con-
> ditions.

As writing teachers, we must speak out for valid assessment and
let the public know about unacceptable conditions. But at times, we
and our students may be stuck with a bad assessment. Even then,
some teachers have managed to call on their creative thinking to
transform the unacceptable.

The Writing Improvement Team at Beaumont High School was
facing the city's pressure for mastery learning in the classroom and
measurable gains on standardized achievement tests. Asenath Lakes
protested, waited, then worried. Finally, recalling a course she'd taken
in software for graphs, charts, and statistics, she devised a demonstration as slick as that of any sales consultant. For a few weeks, she
would collect each student's rough draft, assign a quick holistic score,
and record it as a "pretest." Her "intervention," of course, was a
process approach: peer response, conferencing, editing at the computer.
Then she read the final papers, recording each score as a "posttest."
She used her software to enter the data. At the next department
meeting, a giant graph displayed the results of her experiment in
"mastery learning": a red line showed her students' shabby performance on the pretest, and a green line showed their dramatic gains
when guided through the processes of writing!

Writing Across the Curriculum

To make a real impact on writing performance, a Writing Improvement
Team should reach across the curriculum. Lindbergh began with the
English department, and then the WIT provided an inservice for
teachers of all subjects. Other schools plan an interdisciplinary program
from the start. At Wydown Middle School, reading teacher Marilyn
McWhorter won a Christa McAuliffe Fellowship to develop a writing
inservice for the whole staff and schoolwide assessment. Two years
later, physical education teacher Annette Casey wrote a grant to
enhance Wydown's athletic program with journals, letter writing, and
an inhouse newspaper.

University City High School's team of English and social studies teachers focused on improving equity and access (see chapter 17). Although the student body was 80 percent black, the white minority tended to be children of college faculty—already literate with print and computer. To counter the stereotypes, the Writing Improvement Team targeted developmental classes for lab access. Pat Holm (English) and Jeannette Ivy (history) guided basic students through joint papers with content from social studies and both teachers supporting the processes of writing.

Langston Middle School launched a computer-equipped writing program with an inservice for the whole faculty. The WIT—two lab teachers and two administrators—asked me to plan a three-hour workshop to be held on a Thursday and Friday evening in April. My first thought was, "Who would go out on a Friday night to hear me?" But on the appointed days, twenty-five teachers of classes that included industrial arts and special education came to the lab and wrote at the keyboard. What was the catalyst for Langston's writing across the curriculum?

First was the power of good leadership. Principal Jim Strughold and Instructional Coordinator Christine George attended both sessions of the workshop, brought refreshments, and stayed to write and publish with their faculty.

Next was the power of computers to glamorize and promote writing. Soon, industrial arts students were typing instructions for hanging bulletin boards level, and counselors were helping angry teenagers write through conflicts on the playground.

Such real-world uses of writing are new to most educators. One way to support them is by pairing an English teacher with a colleague from another department to plan for writing-to-learn. Michael Lowenstein led such a project at Harris-Stowe State College, funded by the National Endowment for the Humanities. He spent two years in partnership with a professor of biology, Terry Werner (faculty from English and math formed a second team). The same students enrolled in both classes, scheduled in tandem. Joint projects were designed— the biology class helped students use their senses to observe experiments, and the composition class gave response to lab reports-in-progress. Some readings discussed in English were drawn from biology, and a speakers' series was entitled, "Nature to the poet and to the scientist." The collaboration had a lasting impact on the faculty involved.

Diane Balestri (1986) designed a similar project at Bryn Mawr College, focusing the partnership on writing and computers. A group of students enrolled concurrently in her freshman composition course and her partner's course in PASCAL programming. The two teachers planned together, building a common set of metaphors: students would "revise" a program to refine its "style" and "structure"; they would "debug" an essay until it would "run" through their response group. Through this collaboration, students began to understand the common thinking processes in two seemingly unlike ways of knowing.

At McCluer High School, an eight-member Writing Improvement Team has discovered the same sort of intellectual challenge, and a new enthusiasm for learning together. The team consists of the English department chair, the assistant principal (himself a former writing project leader), a Writing Project teacher-consultant, and representatives from science, social studies, math, foreign language, and practical/fine arts departments. These teachers attended a writing-across-the-curriculum inservice—thirty hours of reading, sharing, writing, and publishing. The team has made writing truly a schoolwide effort.

As Emily Buckhannon worked with her students in McCluer's lab, she shared with other teachers how the computers reinforced the processes of writing. Soon she noticed a new kind of networking, a subtle "coaching in the workplace." Here's how she and some teachers explain it:

> *E.B.:* "The computer brings people together. English people, history people, science people—suddenly you have something tangible to discuss [adding with a wry grin], instead of 'your curriculum.'"
>
> *T1:* "And when you learn to use the computer you *need* input from somebody else. You know 'I can't do this myself.'"
>
> *E.B.:* "So you ask. Some teacher I've never had a conversation with before will come by my English class and say, 'Hey, I've got this word processor. . . .'"
>
> *T2.:* "Yeah, when we set up our hard disk Charlie came over. He loved to do it."
>
> *T3:* "We have a whole group of friends with MacIntoshes and we're always swapping programs and ideas."
>
> *T2:* "Instead of the cooking club it's the Mac club!"

Notes

1. For more information about the Gateway Writing Project's approach to integrating computers in writing programs, see Selfe, Rodrigues, and Oates

(1989). A fuller description, including the final report to FIPSE on pilot schools and Writing Improvement Teams, may be obtained from GWP at the University of Missouri–St. Louis.

2. Letter from Professor James Gray, University of California–Berkeley, to Directors of the National Writing Project, dated January 2, 1990. Gray had been asked by the National Assessment of Educational Progress to comment on NAEP's objectives and procedures. He urged NWP teachers to protest the use of fifteen-minute timed papers as a measure of student ability to handle the complex processes of writing.

19 A Community of Researchers

Among the basic assumptions of the National Writing Project is that teachers can and should do research:

> Classroom practice and research have generated a substantial body of knowledge on the teaching of writing.
>
> The intuitions of teachers can be a productive guide for field-based research, and practicing teachers can conduct useful studies in their classrooms. (Bay Area Writing Project 1984, 2)

The Center for the Study of Writing describes the goal of this research as changing "effective teachers" into "reflective teachers." By closely observing their own students and seeking answers to their own questions, teachers are empowered.

This kind of inquiry is called *action research*. It "involves participants in self-reflection about their situation, as active partners"; it stresses interviewing, observation, dialogue, and collaboration; it explains events by telling a "story" in "the commonsense language people use to describe and explain human actions" (Elliott 1978). Action research by teachers, I believe, should guide the development of a WritingLand community.

Too many inservice projects make teachers the consumers of theory, research, and prepackaged curricula. And when the latest educational buzzword is silenced, people wonder why a highly-acclaimed method worked so poorly in the classroom. As teachers, we need to take a more active role in promoting the kinds of research we can live with.

Too many university-based studies measure some predetermined skill among large numbers of subjects without telling us enough about the process of acquiring and using that skill. Two decades of case studies have revealed a welcome view of individual writers planning, drafting, and revising their texts. But even this qualitative research has often removed students from the classroom to write for an unfamiliar audience and an unknown purpose. The learning environment is generally ignored.

Too many researchers depend on randomly selected classrooms and on experimental conditions uncontaminated by any context. We don't want to learn from randomly selected teachers but from master teachers. Action research plays a special role in a WritingLand context because new tools prod teachers and students to experiment with new techniques.

Writing Projects are natural sites for collaborative research bringing together university researchers and research-wise practitioners. Action research offers a way for teachers to continue learning, growing, inquiring, and publishing after they leave the intense experience of a summer institute. They can study writing as a process in their own classrooms and computer labs. The findings of their research, drawn from fieldnotes and discussion, can have immense practical value for other teachers.

Glenda Bissex and Richard Bullock (1987) introduce their book of classroom studies in this way:

> By becoming researchers, these teachers take control over their classrooms and professional lives in ways that confound the traditional definition of *teacher* and offer proof that education can reform itself from within. Teachers doing case-study analyses of their students present a powerful challenge to society's preconceptions of the nature of schooling, the role of teachers, and ultimately the seat of power in educational decision making. (xi)

Since this book is the product of research by the teachers of the Gateway Writing Project, I want to end with some of their own reflections on the experience.

———

For Anne Wright, a year of classroom inquiry launched a fleet of publications about her work with computers. Active in the Gateway Writing Project since 1978, she had served as codirector in the mid-1980s and published an essay on holistic evaluation (1981). But she didn't think of herself as a scholar. Anne Wright is the sort of person who keeps the local English teachers' association running, who does the organizing but stays out of the limelight, who tends to underestimate her own originality.

Using computers in Hazelwood West's new tutorial writing lab suddenly put her in the vanguard of her field. During 1984–85 she conducted action research using computers to help her seniors gather data for their research papers. After some exploratory reading, students made a "preliminary question outline." One group was asked to record their notes on a simple database; another typed their notes directly on the word processor. Here's what their teacher learned by observing the process:

> The word processing method is preferable to the [database] method

> for several reasons. First, PFS File allows a student to answer only one question on a sheet. The notes on the various questions, then, come printed out on lots of separate sheets and are not as easy to follow. Handwritten notecards are easier to organize. Also, PFS File cannot be integrated directly into PFS Write . . . material [has] to be recopied. The thing PFS did best was make it very clear when bibliographic information on sources was missing, because the prompts were on the screen.

Her comments remind me of my own frustration programing sentence expansion in BASIC. They preview much that we have confirmed after trying some specialized software. Word processing tends to be more flexible, more suited to natural composing. (Databases have great potential for manipulating data in collaborative projects, but for note taking their power wasn't helpful.)

By contrast, the clients of Hazelwood's WritingLand were delighted when word processing eliminated the copying (and miscopying) of the same quotes from draft to draft:

> Once the outline [is typed], all the notes could be written directly below the appropriate question . . . which certainly makes preparing the first draft easier. . . . Once the first draft is on the disk, no other complete drafts have to be written. The first one can be revised as much as time allows. In other words, once the notes have been typed in, they never have to be typed again. Changes and corrections can be made at any stage without complete rewriting. What a time and effort saver!

> Only one of my students actually did his whole paper . . . [on the computer], and he wrote on his own computer at home. The others did not have enough computer time to do it. But I hadn't expected them to. I just wanted them to realize the potential of a computer in this long process.

As her lab became recognized as a model, Wright was asked to give presentations to other schools. Colleagues urged her to try for larger conferences and journals. Gradually she began realizing some of the strengths of her own writing: it is straightforward, clear, practical, and very well informed.

Anne Wright has now published articles in *English Journal,* the *Writing Lab Newsletter, Writing Center Journal,* and the *Quarterly of the National Writing Project/Center for the Study of Writing,* as well as chapters in Pamela Farrell's (1989) book on writing labs. In her research, she applies still-tentative theories in a still-evolving context, then reflects on what happens, and then shares it with a wider audience.

For Joan Krater Thomas, action research has meant planning and leading an ambitious collaborative investigation. She asked why most African-American writers in her integrated, middle-income suburb continued to score low on the annual holistic assessment. With a team of secondary teachers, most of them Writing Project-trained, she wrote a Missouri Incentives for Excellence grant to support their work.

For their first task, they defined the problem by analyzing errors and strengths in several hundred writing samples. I helped with this analysis, which showed that even the lowest-scoring writers seldom used dialect features. Instead, a disproportionate number of black students wrote weak papers, and their writing showed the full range of weaknesses in content and development as well as form.

The solution seemed to lie in carefully tailored approaches to the writing process. From their own experience and from published studies, they chose six teaching principles (such as collaborative learning and building on oral language strengths) which held promise for underachieving black writers. By applying these principles, they found that the computer reinforced all of them and played a role in many successful lessons; the research team revised their list of principles to add, "Use the computer as a writing tool."

Since 1987, each teacher has documented the progress of two or three target students in her own classes. The team has met monthly to share fieldnotes, insights, and problems. Sandy Tabscott was pleased with Shana's poetry essay, which went through many revisions on the computer. The project

> required synthesis of some research plus a personal response to a couple of poems. My words were, "I don't want something you copied out of a book. I want your response. It should have the voice that tells me a real living, breathing person has read and reacted." Shana's paper on Paul Laurence Dunbar was fresh: "He wrote with a slave's dialect, instead of in standard English like we do now. . . . He is a good example of an achieved black poet who used his poetry talent to make his mother proud."

> I had asked myself in February if Shana, who uses and relies on the process so well, was learning anything that would stand her in good stead for the one-shot assessment. The answer is "Yes." Her [test] paper had voice, audience awareness, transitions, full intro and conclusion, sensory and concrete details. It was two pages long and almost error-free. She went from a 4 in the fall to a 14 in May.

Case study writers showed more motivation at the computer than when writing by hand, and were much more willing to stay on task and attempt revision. They also welcomed new technology for modeling process and product. Nancy Cason often used a computer linked to a big television to lead the whole class in collaborative composing:

> During a lesson on vivid detail, [each student] wrote one sentence about the blooming lilac tree outside of our classroom. I synthesized their sentences into verse form as the students watched and offered suggestions. The final product was excellent.

On another occasion, she enlisted the help of Principal Paul Fredstrom to demonstrate the writing process:

> He was working on the eighth draft of a presentation. [The typed, double-spaced draft] was filled with red, blue, and green marks, arrows, scratchouts, etc. I shared his work with the class. When it was finally done, he came and gave them the presentation. This demonstrated to all students that no one, not even the principal, writes his best alone, without feedback, without discussion and thought.

At the end of the first year, the Webster Groves writing assessment showed an 11 percent gain on the 16-point rubric among the eighteen case studies; the second year's gain was an impressive 18 percent. During the third year, these teachers have applied what they learned to larger numbers of basic writers, both black and white, with a closer look at computers to reinforce the processes of writing. This time, the 194 students identified as at-risk—roughly a quarter of each teacher's classes—averaged a 17 percent gain on the year's assessment.

Students are coinvestigators in action research. For some, this role can be mildly amusing or mildly annoying. But for students who have been deeply involved, it can be a very special experience. Let's look at action research through the eyes of one case study writer.

Imani, a sixth grader in Margaret Hasse's room, was especially proud of the fat University log she received for her fieldnotes. She used it spontaneously like a dialogue journal. Once she ended a page by drawing a big heart labeled "Friends Forever." Often she wrote messages which I would answer:

> I took a test in Multiplying and I was on my last one, but gollygee, I got an 100% on it and I get to check other peoples paper too.

Imani experimented with style, trying out more mature language before she could fully manage the context and connotation. For example, she wrote in her journal why she liked working on the case studies: *The ways I cope with you are so interesting to me at times because we get to cut classes some of the time.*

The case study writers enjoyed not only the occasional class breaks, but also the attention from an outsider and from their classmates. The gold-stamped UMSL logs became a sort of status symbol. For weeks after the notebooks arrived, children would stop me in the halls to ask, "How did so-and-so get that book?" and "I just want to know where I can get one of those logs!"

In much the same way, the COMPTRACE program appealed to students who helped with the composing-process research. I've already noted how Bob took personal charge of the software, showing me when it was not working right and suggesting I use a write-protect tape to avoid losing his drafts. Sometimes classmates would stay during lunch or recess to watch as COMPTRACE replayed a friend's composing session.

Recording their data with logs and software gave the case study writers group membership in the Gateway Writing Project and a share in the professionalism of their teachers' research team.

In action research, both students and teachers grow. As Minnie Phillips says of the Webster Groves study,

> Before we identified them, our target students were like Ellison's Invisible Man: faceless kids distinguished more by their failure than their humanity. Putting names with faces and faces with personalities was the key that opened the door to their potential. . . . We are piloting a grassroots approach that might be helpful to other teachers as out of the shadows emerge students, both black and white, whose success may depend on us.

Research on issues they care about by the people who have a stake in the results creates a community of learners—the citizens of WritingLand. When research is a regular part of the classroom agenda, a new energy flows. There is a new integrity in a writing program where students and teachers and administrators and researchers are all engaged in writing. Classroom action research rings true.

Think back to the question that began this section, "Who rules a WritingLand?" Perhaps the best answer is, "a community of writers."

V Explorations

20 Methods of Action Research

Since 1984, the Gateway Writing Project has been documenting the progress of elementary, secondary, and college students who write with computers. Our work is unusual in that it focuses on teachers, writers, and classrooms, not on technology.

While I have avoided academic rituals in telling my story, at this point I need to describe our methods and history in some detail. This chapter is addressed to readers who may be planning action research or those who must assess the validity of the work I've been reporting.

Gateway has been active as a National Writing Project site since 1978, offering summer institutes in process approaches to writing and helping good teachers become workshop leaders, authors, and curriculum developers. By the mid-1980s, the schools we served were buying labs full of microcomputers, with little guidance for teachers on how to use them well.

We wanted our courses to incorporate word processing in a way that retained our focus on the direct experience of writing. But what would be the structure, the content, of such an institute? How to teach what we did not yet know?

Teacher Researchers

We decided to invite the strongest graduates of the Gateway Writing Project back to the University of Missouri–St. Louis for a new summer institute on writing with computers. For an intensive four weeks, they wrote daily, sometimes with pen and paper, sometimes with computers. They reflected on their own experience with different writing tools. And they delved into the emerging research on word processing and writing.

Ten of these teachers received fellowships from the National Writing Project for 1984–85 to study the impact of computers on their own writing classes. They documented how their teaching changed and how their students' writing changed. For one target class, they kept writing folders as well as logs of assignments, problems, successes, and student responses to the computer.

Teachers on this research team welcomed me into their classrooms as a participant-observer. They already knew how to organize and teach a writing workshop. Now they experimented with making the computer a natural part of these workshops, and I watched in their classrooms, writing fieldnotes. Their administrators provided released time for them to meet with me and share what they found.

It has become common in naturalistic research (such as Graves 1975) to present a few sharply focused portraits shading into a group scene in the background. In the same way, our detailed case studies of sixth-graders were developed in a widening context: first Peggy Ryan's classroom, then the four sixth-grade groups, and then all ten classes ranging from grades 3 to 12. This design helped us see how the computer might interact with the culture of varied classrooms.

In subsequent years, our inquiry expanded further still. The Fund for Improvement of Postsecondary Education provided a major grant from 1984–87; this supported continued action research and the formation of Writing Improvement Teams to develop the leadership model. A new National Writing Project grant in 1987–88 brought a partnership with Harris-Stowe State College, the historically black school of education in St. Louis; with the help of Harris-Stowe's Sue Yost, more urban and more elementary teachers entered the picture.

During these years, we looked beyond the classroom to the total school context. The action research focused on pilot schools with Writing Project teachers—middle schools and senior highs, in affluent and modest suburbs as well as in the urban core. At the pilot schools, I worked with my sociologist colleague from the University of Missouri–St. Louis, George McCall. We visited classes, observed student writers, and planned with Writing Improvement Teams of teachers and administrators. The pilot schools have been a natural laboratory for watching the growth and development of computer-equipped writing programs.

Each year, the experience of our teacher-researchers grows, adding to the content and solidity of each new summer institute. Now, when I tell about an idea, I can show it in practice in one of the WritingLands. Finally, in our staff development courses, I feel that we're teaching what we know. Our own research is now at the heart of the Gateway Writing Project.

Most of this research has been qualitative rather than quantitative. That is, we were not out to prove with statistics that writing with computers is better than writing by hand, or that our method of teaching writing is better than Brand X. At the time we began we did not have a "method." Instead, we worked with inquiring teachers to discover and describe good methods in the context of successful writing workshops. Action research is a technical name for this approach.

Action Research

Action research does not begin with fixed hypotheses and tests. Instead, the practical needs of participants generate the research questions, which gain focus in the process of inquiry.

The study takes place in a working environment, not in a laboratory or other sterile setting. Usually practitioners and scholars collaborate as equals.

Action research is ideal for a study of writing with computers. We are dealing with rapidly-changing technology in an evolving social environment, where researchers can't hope to find all the answers and where even the right questions may become apparent only in the classroom.

During the past five years, our studies have generated enough data to fill all too many notebooks and file cabinets and floppy disks. This seems to be typical of action research—it is messy, eclectic, at its best "rich" rather than "concise." Our data were gathered by three quite different methods: case study, ethnography, and experiment.

Case Study

Case studies have been the mainstay of current research on writing. In 1969, when Janet Emig wrote her Harvard dissertation on the composing processes of eight high school seniors (Emig 1971), it seemed revolutionary to study seriously how individual writers who were not professionals went about their work. What Emig learned from interviewing and watching these students, however, challenged the conventional wisdom of the textbooks.

Since then, case study research has revealed the act of writing as students of all ages really experience it, from Donald Graves's work with second graders (1975) to Lillian Bridwell's studies of advanced writers in college (1985). When I took courses with James Britton and Frank Smith at the Ontario Institute for Studies in Education in the mid-1980s, it was the case study research that convinced me to adopt a process approach in my own teaching.

Case studies have been central to action research in the Gateway Writing Project. Classroom teachers interviewed their elementary, secondary, and college writers, observed them in the process of writing by hand or by machine, and examined drafts or printouts. These portraits were collected to form a collage of writers at work. My own focus during one school year was on two sixth graders whose case studies appear in chapters 3 and 4.

Ethnography

Ethnography brings the anthropologist's eye to the classroom. Ethnographers talk about the "culture" and "community" they see, and the "fieldnotes" where they record snatches of dialogue and careful description. Once I realized that this study should not focus on computers but on classrooms, I knew I wanted to do ethnography. To develop some skills, I studied with Lou Smith (Washington University), read Glaser and Strauss (1967) and McCall and Simmons (1969), and took part in the annual Ethnography in Education Research Forum at the University of Pennsylvania.

Feeling like Margaret Mead on some exotic island, I watched students as they wrote in journals, talked with peers, or collaborated at the keyboard. In the evenings, I would read over my notes and start to synthesize, drafting interpretive memos on my computer. At the same time, the teachers who were my co-researchers would be reading over the notes jotted in their logs between classes and writing their own interpretations.

Ethnography is complex. It tries to be true to the perspectives of the culture it describes, not just to the outside observer. So during our monthly meetings we "triangulated" the data: we compared my fieldnotes with the reflections of teachers and students as well as with audiotapes and videotapes of classroom life. The results of this ethnographic observation form the mainstay of this book.

Experimental Research

Though the bulk of our research was descriptive, we used experimental methods and measurements when appropriate. Student writing samples were collected and scored holistically for overall quality, using the methods described by White (1985) and Myers (1980). Words were counted to measure the difference in fluency between papers written by hand and by machine. Changes in content, style, and correctness were counted to see how students applied the power of the computer to revision. Chapters 8 and 9 explain what happened when we asked three groups of students to revise the same story, some with pen and paper, some with the computer. The results turned out to be statistically significant, but the point of the experiment is not the one I started out to prove.

Now if our research had been strictly experimental, I would just have reported the differences between the two writing tools. But action research allows for gradual focusing and refocusing in the process of inquiry. It let me use my new insights to revise my questions—to look beyond the writing tool to the writing teacher. The new hypothesis, that three styles of revision were flourishing in three different classes, was then tested and found statistically significant. The Harry experiment was possible only within the framework of action research.

Multiple Operationalism

During five years of study, we gathered data from many sources using all three methods. While I know that mixing methods is risky, a careful mix can be powerful. Scholars as diverse as Lou Smith (1979) in qualitative research and Campbell and Stanley (1963) in experimental design favor "multiple operationalism"—exploring one question from many angles—to validate key findings. Table 7 shows the data we gathered through each method: case study, ethnography, and quasi-experiment.

Reflexivity

The experience of action research means playing many roles in many contexts. As Hammersley and Atkinson (1983) say in their rationale for ethnography, a researcher is inevitably part of the data. If I try to be a fly on a classroom wall, I'll probably meet a janitor with a can of repellent and a student catching specimens for a science project.

Often experimental research simply ignores the role of the researcher or the impact of the research on the subjects. Yet writers in a laboratory may not give a valid picture of normal writing behavior. (See Don Murray's 1983 report of his life as a "laboratory rat" in Carol Berkenkotter's study of his composing process!) In action research, we observe ourselves along with our subjects, and our interaction with them is a significant part of our data.

In this study, I was observing teachers, who may once have been my students or coauthors, and who now taught me. They, in turn, were observing and learning from their own students while also teaching them. As a research team, we worked together to study a

Table 7
Action Research: Methods and Data in Study of WritingLands

Research Method	Data
Case Study	Taped interviews
	Writing folders
	Sets of drafts and printouts
	Keystroke records (individuals)
	Student logs and reflections
	Standardized test scores
	Affective trait scales
Ethnography	Fieldnotes of classroom observation
	Conferences with teachers
	Teacher logs, reflections
	Videotapes of student interaction
	Keystroke records and audiotapes (collaborative writing)
	Student letters (attitudes on computers and composing)
	Teacher-planned lessons & sequences
Quasi-Experiment	Group statistics on structured revision task (n = 61):
	Holistic scores—revised text
	Holistic scores—pretest
	Fluency measure (word count)
	Error analysis
	Multiple-linear regression analysis of revision types

new phenomenon—the WritingLand—which didn't even exist when we began. Unlike the fly on the wall, we took part in planning and governing the environments we were watching.

I've said in chapter 19 that action research helps the participants grow. And growth means change. The Gateway Writing Project's five-year inquiry into computers and writing has changed our teacher-researchers, just as their work has changed the case study writers. I, too, am not the same researcher I was at the start of this enterprise.

Action research has taught us to observe and tinker—then to step back from our data and ask what it all means. The research we write often has the feel of the personal essay or of feature journalism, showing the process of inquiry as well as the finished product.

Writing this book has been a natural response to the action research. Like a traveler poring through snapshots and souvenirs, I've gone back through my fieldnotes, through the teacher logs, through the student papers. I've relived the experience, and then stepped back to reflect on what it all means and how the pieces fit together. The process of research is simply a process of writing: from observing and arranging, through drafting and peer response and editing, to a publication for a real audience.

I offer this as a more accurate, though still tentative, map to the territory of WritingLand—minus a few electronic monsters, plus a few flesh-and-blood heroes and rulers.

Appendix:
Contributors to the
Action Research

The following lists acknowledge the essential contributions of Gateway Writing Project members to this project. The first list names individual teachers whose work was described or quoted. The second names Writing Improvement Teams of participating schools.

Teachers

Name	Position/School(s)	Chapter(s)
Georgia Archibald	Language Arts Teacher, gifted Steger Sixth Grade Center, Webster Groves Schools (Now Director, The Network)	6; 9
Lillian Atchison	Librarian, University City High	10; 12
Betty Barro	English Teacher Orchard Farm Middle	10; 14
Cathy Beck	English Teacher Hixson Junior High Webster Groves Schools	5
Lori Brandman	Teacher Highcroft Elementary Parkway Schools, Chesterfield	1
Barbara Brooks	English Teacher Writing Center Director Pattonville High	10; 12
Emily Buckhannon	Writing Coordinator McCluer High Ferguson-Florissant Schools	15; 18
Nancy Cason	English Teacher Hixson Junior High Webster Groves Schools	13; 19

Jacqueline Collier	Writing Enrichment Lab Teacher Langston Middle St. Louis Public Schools	10; 15
James Conway	Chair, English Dept. Lindbergh High Sappington, MO	18
Marilyn Dell'Orco	English Teacher, Sacred Heart, Florissant Archdiocese of St. Louis	13
Rochelle Ferdman	Teacher Highcroft Elementary Parkway Schools, Chesterfield	10; 15
Sallyanne Fitzgerald	Director, Center for Academic Development U. of Missouri–St.Louis	14
Bruce Hanan	Chair, English Dept. McCluer High Ferguson-Florissant Schools	1
Margaet Hasse	Teacher Steger Sixth Grade Center Webster Groves Schools (Now retired)	9; 19
Brad Heger	English Teacher, Horton Watkins High Ladue Schools (Now Asst. Principal)	5
Carol Henderson	Writing Enrichment Lab Teacher Clark Elementary St. Louis Public Schools	1; 15
Carolyn Henly	English Teacher Webster Groves High	5
Pat Holm	English Teacher University City High	18
Beverly Hopkins	English Teacher McCluer High Ferguson-Florissant Schools	1; 13

Michael Hopkins	Writing Center Coordinator Parkway South High Chesterfield	17
Joann Hynes	Reading Teacher Pattonville Positive School (Now Pattonville High)	6; 12
Jeannette Ivy	Social Studies Teacher University City High	18
Mary Ann Kelly	English Teacher Hixson Junior High, Webster Groves	5
Asenath Lakes	English Teacher Beaumont High St. Louis Public Schools	14; 18
Michael Lowenstein	Professor, English Harris-Stowe State College St. Louis	18
Chris Madigan	Asst. Professor, English U. of New Mexico, Albuquerque (Now consultant, computers, technical writing)	10; 14
George McCall	Professor, Sociology U. of Missouri–St. Louis	20
Clara McCrary	Teacher, Hawthorne Elem. (Now Flynn Park Elem., Co-Principal Investigator, SEER: Science Ed. Equity Reform) University City Schools	1; 6; 11; 19
Susan Morice	Lecturer, GWP Program Director U. of Missouri–St. Louis (Now Teacher, Wydown Middle Clayton Schools)	6; 10
Norma Owen	Reading/Language Arts Teacher Kirkwood North Middle Kirkwood Schools	6; 9; 13
Michael Pfefferkorn	Chair, Social Studies Dept. Southwest High St. Louis Public Schools	13

Beverly Phillips	Art Teacher, Peabody Elementary St. Louis Public Schools	13
Minnie Phillips	English Teacher, Webster Groves High	19
Margaret Ryan	Language Arts Teacher, St. Jerome's Elementary (Now St. Gregory's Elem. Archdiocese of St. Louis)	Intro.; 2–6; 9; 12
Georgia Schoeffel	Chair, Communications Dept. Southwest High St. Louis Public Schools	15; 18
Roslynde Scott	Writing Enrichment Lab Teacher Ford Middle St. Louis Public Schools	6
Theresa Simon	English Teacher Webster Groves High	14
Sandy Tabscott	English Teacher Hixson Junior High Webster Groves Schools	19
Gail Taylor	English Teacher Hixson Junior High Webster Groves Schools	14
Joan Krater Thomas	Chair, English Hixson Junior High Webster Groves Schools	1; 5; 6; 14; 15; 19
John Weiss	English Teacher Lindbergh High Sappington	6; 12; 14
Terence Werner	Professor, Biology Harris-Stowe State College St. Louis	18
Anne Wright	Writing Lab Director English Teacher Hazelwood West High	1; 5; 10; 12; 14; 15; 19
Susan Yost	Asst. Professor, English Director, Student Support Services Title III, Harris-Stowe State College St. Louis	20

Writing Improvement Teams

School and Members	*Chapter*

Beaumont High   14; 18
St. Louis Public Schools
Ruby Jones, Chair, Communications
Asenath Lakes, Writing Enrichment Lab
Addie Jackson, Communications

Ford Middle   6
St. Louis Public Schools
Madonna Beard, Instructional Coordinator
Roslynde Scott, Writing Enrichment Lab
Lois Hart, Language Arts
Auvelia Arnold, Language Arts
Gwendolyn Brown, Reading

Jackson Park Elementary   10
University City Schools
Dr. Deborah Holmes, Principal
(Now Principal, Brittany Woods Middle)
Staff
Parent volunteers

Langston Middle   10; 15; 18
St. Louis Public Schools
James Strughold, Principal
Christine George, Instr. Coord.
Jacqueline Collier, Enrichment Lab
Lynette Williams, Enrichment Lab
Barbara Brown, Language Arts

Lindbergh High   11; 17; 18
Lindbergh Schools, Sappington, MO
Cynthia Jaskowiak, Principal
James Conway, Chair, English
John Weiss, English
Christy Holmes, English
Mary Ann Fanter, English

McCluer High   1; 15; 18
Ferguson-Florissant Schools
Michael Thacker, Asst. Principal
Bruce Hanan, Chair, English
Emily Buckhannon, Writing Coordinator
Faculty representatives from art, business, foreign
languages, home economics, library media, math, music,
physical ed., science, social studies.

Orchard Farm Middle   10; 14
Orchard Farm Schools
Jeanne Dunkmann, Language Arts Coordinator
Betty Barro, English
Dr. Gary Van Meter, Superintendent

Parkway South High   17
Parkway Schools, Chesterfield, MO
Dr. Patrick Berger, Chair, English
Michael Hopkins, Writing Center Coordinator
James Leible, English

Southwest High   15; 18
St. Louis Public Schools
Thomas Daly, Principal
Georgia Schoeffel, Chair, Communications
Michael Pfefferkorn, Chair, Social Studies

Steger Sixth Grade Center   9; 16; 19
Webster Groves Schools
Dr. Donald Morrison, Principal
Georgia Archibald, Language Arts, Gifted
Margaret Hasse, Language Arts
Ed Redden, Language Arts/Social Studies

University City High   10; 12; 18
University City Schools
Andrea Tkach, Chair, English
Lillian Atchison, Librarian
Pat Holm, English
James Schwantes, English
Jeannette Ivy, Social Studies
Bertha Smith, Social Studies

Webster Groves School District Action Research Team   5; 12–15
Hixson Junior & Webster Groves High
Paul Fredstrom, Hixson Principal
Joan Krater Thomas, Hixson Chair, English
Cathy Beck, Hixson, English
Nancy Cason, Hixson, English
Mary Ann Kelly, Hixson, English
Sandy Tabscott, Hixson, English
Gail Taylor, Hixson, English
Carolyn Henly, WGHS, English
Minnie Phillips, WGHS, English
Theresa Simon, WGHS, English
Stephanie Gavin, Hixson, English

Wydown Middle   6; 18
Clayton Schools
Jere Hochman, Principal
Marilyn McWhorter, Reading/English
Rosemarie Fleming, English
Susan Morice, English
Annette Casey, Physical Education

The Gateway Writing Project
Dr. Jane Zeni,
University of Missouri–St. Louis, Director
Dr. Michael Lowenstein,
Harris-Stowe State College, Codirector
Georgia Schoeffel,
St. Louis Public Schools, Codirector

Bibliography

Archibald, G., Spina, L., Krater, J., & Flinn, J. Z. (Eds.) (1984). *New routes to writing, K–8*. St. Louis: Gateway Writing Project (National Council of Teachers of English).

Arms, V. M. (1983). Creating and recreating. *College Composition and Communication, 34*, 355–58.

Arms, V. M. (1988). The right answer to the wrong question. *Computers and Composition, 6* (1), 33–46.

Atwell, N. (1987). *In the middle: Writing, reading, and learning with adolescents*. Upper Montclair, NJ: Boynton/Cook.

Balestri, D. (1987). Algorithms and arguments: A programming metaphor for composition. In L. Gerrard (Ed.), *Writing at century's end: Essays on computer-assisted composition* (pp. 36–44). New York: Random House.

Barrs, M. (1983). The new orthodoxy about writing: Confusing process and pedagogy. *Language Arts, 60* (7), 829–840.

Bay Area Writing Project. (1984). [Brochure].

Bernhardt, S. A., & Appleby, B. C. (1985). Collaboration in professional writing with the computer: Results of a survey. *Computers and Composition, 3* (1), 29–42.

Bissex, G., & Bullock, R. (1987). *Seeing for ourselves: Case-study research by teachers of writing*. Portsmouth, NH: Heinemann.

Bollefer, B., Johnston, L., & Phillips, B. (1988). Publishing. In J. Z. Flinn, G. Schoeffel, & M. Lowenstein (Eds.), *Curriculum strategies: Teaching writing with computers* (Vol. 5, pp. 124–34). St. Louis: Gateway Writing Project.

Brand, A. (1987). Hot cognition: Emotions and writing behavior. *Journal of Advanced Composition, 6*, 5–15.

Bridwell, L. S. (1980). Revising strategies in twelfth grade students' transactional writing. *Research in the Teaching of English, 14*, 197–222.

Bridwell, L. S., Sirc, G., & Brooke, R. (1985). Revising and computing: Case studies of student writers. In S. Freedman (Ed.), *The acquisition of writing language: Revision and response*. Norwood, NJ: Ablex.

Britton, J. (1967). *Talking and writing*. London: Methuen.

Britton, J. (1970). *Language and learning*. New York: Penguin.

Britton, J., Burgess, T., Martin, N., McLeod, A., & Rosen, H. (1975). *The development of writing abilities (11–18)*. London: Macmillan.

Brooks, B. (1989). Scheduling. In P. Farrell (Ed.), *High school writing center: Establishing and maintaining one* (pp. 45–54). Urbana, IL: National Council of Teachers of English.

Bruffee, K. (1983). Writing and reading as collaborative acts. In J. N. Hays, P. A. Roth, J. R. Ramsey, & R. D. Foulke (Eds.), *The writer's mind: Writing as a mode of thinking* (pp. 159–169). Urbana, IL: National Council of Teachers of English.

Calkins, L. M. (1980). Notes and Comments: Children's rewriting strategies. *Research in the Teaching of English, 14,* 330–41.

Calkins, L. M. (1983). *Lessons from a child.* Portsmouth, NH: Heinemann-Boynton/Cook.

Calkins, L. M. (1986). *The art of teaching writing.* Portsmouth, NH: Heinemann.

Campbell, D. T., & Stanley, J. C. (1963). Experimental and quasi-experimental designs for research in teaching. In N. L. Gage (Ed.), *Handbook of research on teaching.* Chicago: Rand-McNally.

Collier, R. (1983). The word processor and revision strategies. *College Composition and Communication, 34,* 149–155.

Collins, J., & Sommers, E. (Eds.) (1985). *Writing on-line: Using computers in the teaching of writing.* Upper Montclair, NJ: Boynton/Cook.

Daiute, C. (1985). *Writing and computers.* Reading, MA: Addison-Wesley.

Dell'Orco, M. (1985). God, what hath DOS wrought? National Catholic Education Association Annual Meeting, St. Louis, April 7.

Dewey, J. (1967 [1916]). *Democracy and education.* New York: Free Press.

Ehrmann, S., & Balestri, D. (Eds. for the FIPSE Technology Study Group). (1987). Learning to design, designing to learn: A more creative role for technology. *Machine-Mediated Learning, 2(1&2),* 9–33.

Elbow, P. (1973). *Writing without teachers.* New York: Oxford.

Elliott, H. (1978). What is action research? Paper presented at the annual conference of the Classroom Action Research Network, Cambridge, England.

Emig, J. (1971). *The composing processes of twelfth graders.* Urbana, IL: National Council of Teachers of English.

Farrell, P. (Ed.) (1989). *The high school writing center: Establishing and maintaining one.* Urbana, IL: National Council of Teachers of English.

FIPSE Technology Study Group, D. Balestri, Chair. (1988). *Ivory towers, silicon basements: Learner-centered computing in postsecondary education.* McKinney, TX: Academic Computing/EDUCOM.

Fitzgerald, S. (1988). Relationships between conferencing and movement between general and specific in basic writers' compositions. *Dissertation Abstracts International, 48,* 3040A. (University Microfilms No. 88-01,617).

Flinn, J. Zeni (1986a). Composing, computers, and contexts: Case studies of revision among sixth graders in National Writing Project classrooms. *Dissertation Abstracts International, 46,* 3636A. (University Microfilms No. 86-02,959).

Flinn, J. Zeni (1986b). *The role of instruction in revising with computers: Forming a construct for "good writing."* St. Louis, MO: University of Missouri-St. Louis, Gateway Writing Project. (ERIC Document Reproduction Service No. ED 274-963)

Flinn, J. Zeni (1987a). Case studies of revision aided by keystroke recording and replaying software; Programming software to trace the composing process. *Computers & Composition, 5* (1), 31–49.

Flinn, J. Zeni (1987b). Computers in the writing process: A rhetoric of tools. *The Quarterly of the National Writing Project and the Center for the Study of Writing, 9 (2),* 24.

Flinn, J. Zeni (1989). Electronic writing: The autobiography of a collaborative adventure. *Quarterly of the National Writing Project/ Center for the Study of Writing, 11* (3), 22–27.

Flinn, J. Zeni, & Madigan, C. (1989a). Gateway writing project: Staff development and computers in St. Louis. In C. Selfe, D. Rodrigues, & W. Oates (Eds.), *Computers in English and Language Arts: The challenge of teacher education.* Urbana, IL: National Council of Teachers of English.

Flinn, J. Zeni, & Madigan, C. (1989b). High-tech staff development. *Writing Program Administration Journal, 12* (3), 21–30.

Florio-Ruane, S. (1986, April). *Taking a closer look at writing conferences.* Presentation at the annual American Educational Research Association, San Francisco. (ERIC Document Reproduction Service No. ED 275-003)

Flower, L. (1989, May). *Studying cognition in context: Introduction to the study.* (Center for the Study of Writing Technical Report No. 21). Berkeley, CA & Pittsburgh, PA: University of California & Carnegie Mellon University.

Flower, L., & Hayes, J. R. (1981). A cognitive process theory of writing. *College Composition and Communication, 32,* 365–87.

Flower, L., Hayes, J. R., Carey, L., Schriver, K., Stratman, J. (1986). Detection, diagnosis, and the strategies of revision. *College Composition and Communication, 37,* 16–55.

Franklin, S., & Madian, J. (Eds.) (1988). *Making the literature, writing, word processing connection: Best of the Writing Notebook.* Mendocino, CA: Creative Word Processing in the Classroom.

Freedman, S. (1987). *Response to student writing.* (NCTE Research Report No. 23). Urbana, IL: National Council of Teachers of English.

Gateway Writing Project (1984, 1985, 1986, 1987, 1988, 1989). *Curriculum strategies: Teaching writing with computers.* 5 annual volumes. Coedited by various colleagues.

Gerrard, L. (1989). Computers and basic writers: A critical view. In G. Hawisher & C. Selfe (Eds.), *Critical perspectives on computers and composition instruction* (pp. 94-108). New York: Teachers College.

Glaser, B. G., & Strauss, A. L. (1967). *The discovery of grounded theory: Strategies for qualitative research.* Chicago: Aldine.

Glatthorn, A. (1981). *Writing in the schools: Improvement through effective leadership.* Reston, VA: National Association of Secondary School Principals.

Golub, Jeff, & others (1988). *Focus on collaborative learning: Classroom practices in teaching English, 1988.* Urbana, IL: National Council of Teachers of English.

Goswami, D., and Stillman, P. (1987). *Reclaiming the classroom: Teacher research as an agency for change.* Upper Montclair, NJ: Boynton/Cook.

Graves, D. (1975). An examination of the writing processes of seven year old children. *Research in the Teaching of English, 9,* 227–41.

Graves, D. (1983). *Writing: Teachers and children at work.* Portsmouth, NH: Heinemann.

Grow, G. (1988). Lessons from the computer writing problems of professionals. *College Composition and Communication, 39,* 217–20.

Hammersley, M., & Atkinson, P. (1983). *Ethnography: Principles in practice.* London, England: Tavistock Publishers.

Hawisher, G. (1989). Research and recommendations for computers and composition. In G. Hawisher & C. Selfe (Eds.), *Critical perspectives on computers and composition instruction* (pp. 44–69). New York: Teachers College.

Hawkins, J. (1984). *Computer and girls: Rethinking the issues* (Tech. Rep. No. 24). New York: Bank Street College of Ed.

Herrmann, A. W. (1987). An ethnographic study of a high school writing class using computers: Marginal, technically proficient, and productive learners. In L. Gerrard (Ed.), *Writing at century's end* (pp. 79–91). New York: Random Hse.

Herrmann, A. W. (1989). Computers in public schools: Are we being realistic? In G. Hawisher & C. Selfe (Eds.), *Critical perspectives on computers and composition instruction* (pp. 109–25). New York: Teachers College.

Hillocks, G. (1986). *Research on written composition.* Urbana, IL: National Council of Teachers of English.

Hull, G., & Smith, W. L. (1985). Error correction and computing. In J. L. Collins & E. A. Sommers (Eds.), *Writing on-line* (pp. 89–101). Upper Montclair, NJ: Boynton/Cook.

Hughes, Langston. 1955. *Selected poems of Langston Hughes.* New York: Alfred A Knopf.

Johnson, D. W., Johnson, R. T., & Holubec, E. J. (1988). *Cooperation in the classroom.* (Rev.) Edina, MN: Interaction Book Co.

Joyce, B., & Showers, B. (1988). *Student achievement through staff development.* New York: Longman.

Kane, J. (1983). *Computers for composing* (Tech. Rep. No. 21).New York: Bank Street College of Education.

Krater, J. (1981). Make a mess, Polish a paper. In J. Z. Flinn (Ed.), *Reflections on writing, K–12* (pp. 39–46). St. Louis: Gateway Writing Project (National Council of Teachers of English).

Langer, S. (1942). *Philosophy in a new key.* Cambridge, MA: Harvard.

LeBlanc, P. (1988). How to get the words just right: A reappraisal of word processing and revision. *Computers and Composition, 5*(3), 29–42.

Levin, J., Riel, M., Rowe, R., & Boruta, M. (1985). Muktuk meets Jacuzzi: Computer networks and elementary writers. In S. Freedman (Ed.), *Acquisition of written language: Revision and response* (pp. 160–71). Norwood, NJ: Ablex.

Macrorie, K. (1971). *Writing to be read.* New York: Heinemann-Boynton/Cook.

Madigan, C. (1984). The tools that shape us: Composing by hand vs. composing by machine. *English Education, 16,* 143–50.

Madigan, C., & Sanders, S. (1988). Team planning a computerized technical writing course. *Computers and Composition, 5* (2), 39–50.

McCall, G. J., & Simmons, J. L. (1969). *Issues in participant observation: A text and reader.* Reading, MA: Addison-Wesley.

McCrary, C. (1981). First graders meet Langston Hughes, and they, too sing America. In J. Z. Flinn (Ed.), *Reflections on writing, K–12* (pp. 61-70). St. Louis: Gateway Writing Project (National Council of Teachers of English).

Mehan, H. (1985). *Computers in classrooms: A quasi-experiment in guided change.* (N.I.E. Contract No. 6-83-0027). Washington, DC: National Institute of Education.

Melton, D. (1985). *Written and illustrated by. . . .* Kansas City, MO: Landmark Editions.

Michaels, S. (1986). *The computer as a dependent variable.* (Unpub. research paper.) Cambridge, MA: Harvard Microcomputer and Literacy Project.

Murray, D. (1968). *A writer teaches writing.* Boston: Houghton-Mifflin.

Murray, D. (1978). Internal revision: A process of discovery. In C. Cooper & L. Odell (Eds.), *Research on composing: Points of departure* (pp. 85–104). Urbana, IL: NCTE.

Murray, D. (1983). Response of a laboratory rat—or, being protocoled. *College Composition and Communication, 34,* 169–72.

Murray, D. (1985). *A writer teaches writing* (rev. ed.). Boston: Houghton-Mifflin.

Myers, M. (1980). *A procedure for writing assessment and holistic scoring.* Urbana, IL: National Council of Teachers of English.

National Assessment of Educational Progress (1986). *The writing report card: Results from the fourth National Assessment,* Ed. J. Langer, R. Appleby, & I. Mullis. Princeton, NJ: The College Board.

Newman, D. (1984). *Functional environments for microcomputers in education* (Tech. Rep. No. 25). New York: Bank Street College of Education.

Nichols, R. (1986). Word processing and basic writers. *Journal of Basic Writing, 5,* 81–97.

Papert, S. (1980). *Mindstorms: Children, computers, and powerful ideas.* New York: Basic Books.

Parson, G. (1985). *Hand in hand: The writing process and the microcomputer— Two revolutions in the teaching of writing.* Urbana, IL: National Council of Teachers of English.

Perl, S. (1979). The composing processes of unskilled college writers. *Research in the Teaching of English, 13,* 317–36.

Perl, S., & Wilson, N. (1986). *Through teachers' eyes: Portraits of writing teachers at work.* Portsmouth, NH: Heinemann.

Reagan, S. (1988). Teaching TA's to teach: Show, don't tell. *Writing Program Administration, 11(3),* 41–52.

Rico, G. (1983). *Writing the natural way.* Los Angeles: Tarcher.

Rodrigues, D., & Rodrigues, R. (1986). *Teaching writing with a word processor, Grades 7–13.* Urbana, IL: National Council of Teachers of English.

Scardamalia, M., & Bereiter, C. (1983). Child as co-investigator: Helping children gain insight into their own mental processes. In S. Paris, G. Olson & H. Stevenson (Eds.), *Learning and maturation in the classroom.* Hillsdale, NJ: Erlbaum.

Selfe, C. (1989). Redefining literacy: The multilayered grammars of computers. In G. Hawisher & C. Selfe (Eds.), *Critical perspectives on computers and composition instruction* (pp. 3–15). New York: Teachers College.

Selfe, C.L., Rodrigues, D., and Oates, W.R. 1989. Computers in English and the language arts: The challenge of teacher education. Urbana: NCTE.

Shaughnessy, M. (1977). *Errors and expectations: A guide for the teacher of basic writing.* New York: Oxford.

Sheingold, K., Hawkins, J., and Char, C. (1984). *"I'm the thinkist, you're the typist": The interaction of technology and the social life of classrooms* (Tech. Rep. No. 27). New York: Bank Street College of Education.

Smith, F. (1982). *Writing and the writer.* New York: Holt, Rinehart & Winston.

Smith, L. (1979). An evolving logic of participant observation, educational ethnography, and other case studies. In L. Shulman (Ed.), *Review of research in education* (Vol. 6, pp. 316–77). Chicago: Peacock.

Sommers, N. (1980). Revision strategies of student writers and experienced adult writers. *College Composition and Communication, 31,* 378–88.

Spitzer, M. (1989). Computer conferencing: An emerging technology. In G. Hawisher & C. Selfe (Eds.), *Critical perspectives on computers and composition instruction* (pp. 187–200). New York: Teachers College.

Strong, W. (1986). *Creative approaches to sentence combining.* Urbana, IL: National Council of Teachers of English.

Thomas, J. K. (1989) *Collaborative action research: Improving black student writing.* (Unpub. report). School District of Webster Groves, MO. See also Krater, J.

Turkle, S. (1984). *The second self: Computers and the human spirit.* New York: Simon and Schuster.

Vygotsky, L. (1978). *Mind in society: The development of higher psychological processes.* (M. Cole, V. John-Steiner, S. Scribner, E. Souberman, Eds.). Cambridge, MA: Harvard.

White, E. (1985). *Teaching and assessing writing.* New York: Jossey-Bass.

Withey, M. (1983). The computer and writing. *English Journal, 72* (7), 24-31.

Wright, A. (1981). School writing assessment: A first step toward writing across the curriculum. In J. Z. Flinn (Ed.), *Reflections on writing, K–12* (pp. 75–81). St. Louis: Gateway Writing Project (NCTE).

Wright, A. (1986). "Hazelwood West Writing Lab: A center of excellence." *The Quarterly of the National Writing Project and the Center for the Study of Writing, 8* (3), 10–11.

Wright, A. (1988). Teaching writing while jumping through new technological hoops. *English Journal, 77* (7), 33–38.

Zeni, J. See Flinn, J. Zeni.

Author

Jane Zeni is assistant professor of English and educational studies at the University of Missouri–St. Louis, where she also directs the Gateway Writing Project. From 1984 to 1987, with the help of a major grant from the Fund for Improvement of Postsecondary Education, she developed a program integrating computers into her project's workshops in teaching writing. She took part in the FIPSE Technology Study Group, chairing the teleconference on composition and design in such diverse fields as architecture, music, genetics, programming—and writing. Committed to the writing project goal of a new professionalism, she has edited two books by Gateway teachers, *Reflections on Writing* and, with Archibald, Spina, and Krater, *New Routes to Writing*; both were sponsored by the Greater St. Louis English Teachers' Association and distributed by NCTE. For the past three years she has been assisting a team of secondary teachers in Webster Groves, Missouri, on collaborative action research with at-risk African-American writers. She has published in *Computers and Composition, English Education, Educational Leadership*, the NWP *Quarterly*, and *Writing Program Administration Journal*, formerly under the name Jane Zeni Flinn.